D1519706

*Brooke on her first day of sixth grade, one year
before the accident.*

LOOK **BOTH** WAYS

LOOK **BOTH** WAYS

Brooke Ellison

SMALL BATCH BOOKS
AMHERST, MASSACHUSETTS

Printed in the United States of America

Interior design by Megan Katsanevakis

ISBN 978-1-951568-18-4
Library of Congress Control Number: 2021924474

SMALL
BATCH
BOOKS

493 South Pleasant Street
Amherst, Massachusetts 01002
413.230.3943
SMALLBATCHBOOKS.COM

←——————→

Carter, James, Harrison, Oliver, and Theodore—you are the brightest lights in my life. I dedicate *Look Both Ways* to all of you. It is my hope that the words on these pages and the thoughts behind them will ever be a reminder of how much you are loved and that no matter how near to or far from you I might be, I am always with you, and your voices, smiles, and laughter are nestled into every corner of my heart.

CONTENTS

←——→

PROLOGUE

←——————→

WHEN I FIRST CONCEIVED OF this book, a veritable part two of other things I have written or have been written about me, I was of a mind that it would decidedly not be a book about disability. There are valuable understandings that have come to sit at the very foundation of my identity that I felt are of equal value to anyone; the thoughts I have to share are relevant to a much broader audience than what might be found in the fraction of the population likely to open a book that references "disability." In many ways, I feel that same conviction now, to this day, even as I write this very paragraph.

Bookstore shelves and Amazon search results offer an immense number of biographical and autobiographical texts that are designed to shed some light on the personal transformations people undergo after having experienced a disabling accident or life-changing medical diagnosis. In fact, I am included in this very list of authors whose basis for writing rested solely on the occurrence and aftermath of a paralyzing condition. Often contextualized in terms of "inspiration" or "role-modelhood," many of these stories and deeply personal accounts fill a functional position in a structured society.

The great and prolific social theorist Émile Durkheim envisioned society in just this way: that all social experiences and entities can be thought of in terms of the functions they play in the overall social structure. For instance, if we were to look at the class-based structure of U.S. society, we would have to understand each class in terms of the role it plays in maintaining the status quo, how the functioning of our complex social experiences is defined by the structure that the class system helps to create. Durkheim's structural functionalist model views the organization of society in terms of the roles that communities of people, institutions, systems, and even laws play, and how they give the functioning of society the assistance it needs.

That is an extremely cursory and incomplete description of a well-integrated and well-argued theory of the social experience that Durkheim spent a career developing and volumes articulating. What is more, many subsequent generations of social theory went to considerable lengths redefining, challenging, and sometimes even directly refuting Durkheim's model. Indeed, his is neither the only nor the best sociological framework from which to understand what this experience we casually call "life" is all about. But I do think it offers, at minimum, an insightful standpoint from which to look at disability and the role it has played in social life within the U.S. and beyond.

What does "disability" mean in the context of U.S. society and culture, not just for those who live with disability but for everyone? People who live with disability live in a fascinating existential limbo, simultaneously revered by and repelled from a broader society that wants no more to consider itself disabled than it wants to be accused of neglecting the disabled. It's a one part apotheosis, one part repugnance, one part scared as hell, triadic relationship that makes those living with disability, in many ways, the basis on which others can believe they gain social perspective while, at the same time, climb at least one rung on the social ladder. People living with disability are celebrated yet rejected, are the objects both of praise and of ridicule, and are heralded for their understandings of challenge while often left to battle those challenges on their own.

At least, this is how some, maybe even many, members of the "disability community" view the situation, and not at all for unjustified reasons. There are very few who *want* to be disabled and, as a result, don't want to associate with it. Unlike so many other social characteristics or demographics, disability isn't always or even usually congenital; it's a looming, fate-based wild card that most want to stay as removed from as possible. Disability makes life unquestionably harder, and no one wants life to be harder than it already is. We can appreciate the triumph of human spirit that is born out of continuously battling physical struggle, the "heroism" people associate with the degree of fortitude needed to gut it out day after day, but let us admire that individual resolve in someone else. The problem with these admiration-from-afar notions of disability and its position in society is that it allows us to create a zero-sum, binary understanding of disability: something we either are or aren't. And by virtue of that binary approach, it is so much easier for us to view the concept as something we either do or do not have to pay attention to. Turns out, I am just as guilty of this as is anyone else. Even more importantly, this distancing of oneself from all things considered "disabled" is based on the fundamental misunderstanding that the losses associated with disability come with exactly zero qualifiers, and that the scales of justice by which so many of us heuristically understand our lives use disability to tip the balance toward unfairness. And that simply isn't true.

So, in my initial conception of this book, I thought I would distance myself from references to "disability" and, in so doing, cater to an audience that might likewise want to distance itself from disability. But what value would that provide? My initial intention was that I would share my thoughts and understandings in such a way that they were "all inclusive" by refraining from mentioning disability. The fact of the matter is, though, that these thoughts and understandings are all-inclusive *because of* their reference to disability. That, I hope, is the central theme and takeaway from the book: that to view disability of any kind in terms of who does and does not belong to it is to shortchange everyone. It is to render unprepared a society that can gain not just from having disability as a point of perspective but also from the lessons it forces one to learn that are applicable to everyone. While likely never something to be sought out or desired, disability, whether it is in the form of paralysis, deafness, blindness, or any other -ness, is not something to be feared or distanced from. It is inevitably present in the richness of the human experience, and it has taught me as much about who I am as it has taught me about what we all can endure.

It is impossible for me to disentangle my thoughts and perspectives on the world from the events in my life that have precipitated them. To even attempt to do so would be to eliminate the causal mechanism by which so much of my identity has been formed and would render hollow the sincerity of many of my words. I say that with the fullest admission that I have historically understood myself only very minimally in reference to anything disability-related, and that countless numbers of people can speak very sincerely and meaningfully about lessons about life without having ever experienced its most humbling adversity. For me, however, the lens from which I view the world is not one of *disability* but, rather, one of *humanity touched by disability*, which serves to heighten the lessons so fundamental to our lives: those of adaptation and problem-solving, leadership and growth, compassion and hope. These are the lessons of disability. These are the lessons of life.

In what follows, you can expect an integration of autobiography and a translation from what is singular or personally identifying to what is universal. Inasmuch as it is anecdotal, it is also pluralistic: my life as a case study of many lives. Behind these introductory pages, I plan to use the word "disability" only as much as necessary, which is admittedly frequently, neither running toward nor away from it. It is an identified qualifier for my life, but I am neither diminished nor circumscribed by it.

I am fortunate that my life has been rich with experience—far more experiences than could easily or comprehensively be included in this book, though many of them are. But this is also a compilation of things I have learned and realizations I have come to by virtue of the evolution of my life, and I hope they will mean something to you. I will conclude this introduction with a quotation from one of my favorite writers and thinkers who has also helped me make meaning of life, David Foster Wallace:

The most obvious, ubiquitous, important realities are often the ones that are hardest to see and talk about.

Functionalist theory as a
source of bias

Brooke on the day she returned home from the hospital,
May 21, 1991. Clockwise from left: neighbors Eddie,
Ellen, Eileen, and Suzie O'Connor; Brooke's sister, Kysten,
and brother, Reed.

ORIGINS

The human body is, at once, frighteningly fragile and resolutely resilient.
Our bodies break in ways that our spirit can remain unbroken.

I SHOULD NOT BE HERE. By nearly all medical prognostication and statistical realism, I should not be here. In fact, anyone with any wagering savvy might have placed her chips on someone else. But lives do not always adhere to probabilities, bell curves, or standard deviations. Personal will favors the long game over the short; determination and hopefulness strive for the less likely instead of the more—the extreme rather than the mean.

I have lived for thirty years with quadriplegia, a duration that is, in itself, far outside of the expected. However, the circumstances under which I became quadriplegic reduce the likelihood of this longevity even further.

It was 1990, and I was eleven years old. In what maybe I thought was an idyllic or quintessentially American scene, I was walking home from my first day of junior high school in an unrelentingly charming Long

Island town. The route to my house from my junior high school was transected by a major highway where cars travel fast and pedestrians with trepidation. By foot or car, there was no way to get to my home from my school if not over this highway: The divide has since come to symbolize two different vantage points from which I now understand my life.

I was hit by a car while I was walking home from my first day of seventh grade. Sometimes, to this day, I think I still hear the screeching of the brakes being applied to the car traveling fifty-five miles per hour or the shattering of glass as my head hit the windshield. To this day, more than three decades later, when traveling on that highway, I still look for traces of blood or sheets of loose-leaf paper that may memorialize a point in my life that has been hazily etched in my memory.

Nicolls Road, which cuts north and south across Long Island's Suffolk County, was the river Styx across which Charon could not guarantee my safe passage. Looking north on this road could not present a more tranquil picture: a school and university to the west, a series of churches and a hospital to the east. And on that particular day, a cadre of friends, walking home from school on either side. That day in 1990 and the next several days are captured for me in narrative and lore much more than in actual cognitive memory. I was, by virtue of my accident, the victim of many crimes perpetuated by fate. I was what is anesthetically and cryptically called, at least by emergency medicine experts, a "critical save," in that my body was in respiratory and cardiac arrest at the same time and in need of resuscitation. Couple this with what appeared to be extensive head trauma, nearly certain spinal cord injury, and innumerable broken bones, and the "critical save" status in which emergency responders found me could be characterized much more by its critical nature than the likelihood of saving.

Fragile, profoundly injured, and nearer to death than I was to life, I was brought to the trauma unit of the Stony Brook University Hospital.

It was a series of Herculean medical efforts that pulled me away from the precipice between life and the beyond. When you are a doctor treating a child whose life would otherwise end far too soon, or when you are the parent of a child whose life would end far too soon were it not for that physician, words like "futility" or "long shot" bear no meaning, take up no space in one's mouth. For better or for worse, my life didn't play the odds and knew nothing of futile.[1]

My accident did not result in my death, nor did it leave me with damage to my brain, though both of these would have been likely outcomes—far likelier, actually, than my survival. I am the anomaly—the probability that keeps the gambler at the craps table. My survival was almost entirely the result of happenstance: It took place right outside the Setauket Fire Department, whose firefighters and emergency responders regularly perform debts that no amount of gratitude could ever repay, and they were almost immediately on the scene, administering CPR to bring to life a heart that had gone into cardiac arrest and provide resuscitation to my lungs, which were being starved of oxygen. The emergency responders who were tending to me within minutes of my being thrown over one hundred feet from the hood of a car and onto the pavement, whose intransigence is often underappreciated until it is met face-first, are members of my community whose description as heroes seems trite.

My survival was also the result of the accident having taken place in such proximity to Stony Brook University Hospital, the largest trauma center in Suffolk County, just a few hundred feet from where I lay on the pavement. I was brought to the hospital by ambulance and was taken through the emergency department to the trauma unit: the medical real estate reserved for only the most elite cases, the netherworld where few enter and far fewer leave.

It is a familial nightmare to find yourself waiting outside the swinging doors of a trauma unit, a horror of an experience that no child, and certainly no parent, desires to undergo. For those who are not deeply immersed in the health-care professions, the hospital and all it symbolizes is a terrifying place, where vulnerability is the vernacular and death is omnipresent. My parents sat outside the trauma unit of Stony Brook University Hospital, desperate for answers or information about circumstances they could not comprehend and a prognosis they could not imagine. They were told I had suffered head trauma and that the EEG readings were flat, indicating that it was likely that I would not survive and, if I did, it would be a life not worth living, as my cognitive function would be almost nonexistent. These are the makings of horror stories, the stuff of nightmares.

"You should start preparing yourselves now," my parents were told, as if it were a weather forecast. "You should expect the worst," as if the impact of "the worst" could be diminished through mere expectation.

Much of the grim diagnosis that my parents received—the worst they were told to anticipate—did not come to actuality. My accident did, however, cause injury to my spinal cord—an unimaginably delicate and susceptible part of the body, whose fragile nature is only surpassed by its importance and elegance. A work of art evolved and perfected over millennia, the spinal cord, when it is injured, often results in paralysis from the point of injury down. I don't know what part of my accident created this specific injury, whether it was my head hitting the windshield or my body hitting the ground or the sheer impact of being hit by a car traveling so fast—all of those are possibilities, meaningless at that. What is operative about this is that the injury took place at such a high point of my spinal cord, a subluxation at my second and third vertebrae, that it left me paralyzed from my neck down and unable to breathe on my own.

Those are the facts of the story, the preliminary background research for which I am known but not understood. It is strange when your destiny meets you at such an unexpectedly early point in your life, when the moment for which you think you will be defined is not the product of a lifetime's worth of events but an isolated incident. Our destiny is not measured in the future tense, it is a synonym for what is and sometimes can't be understood. What defines us is really the summation of many nondefining moments. They are happening right now.

Being hit by a car is a modern-day biblical scourge—an incident that occurs rarely enough but whose effects are catastrophic enough to be almost symbolic or allegorical of our vulnerability as human beings. When I was little, I had an intense fear of being hit by a car. When my parents would drop me off at dancing school, I would ask them to drop me off in the parking spot directly in front of the school's entrance so as to avoid the necessity of walking through an ill-lit parking lot at night. Being hit by a car—much like breaking your neck or cracking your head open—was always, to me, merely a colloquialism for meeting your demise.

Being hit by a car is a rarity, and surviving it is even rarer. There is a bit of a fascination, particularly among children (and likely adults as well, though they are often too bound by the principles of decorum to ask), about the details of my accident. People are curious about whether the driver of the car had been drinking. He had not. People want to know if I was the only one injured or if others were as well. This question is far less straightforward, as I was the only one who was physically injured, but undeniably, my accident was traumatic for many more than just me. People want to know what my relationship is with the driver of the car and whether a relationship of unexpected beauty might have grown out of an accident so unequivocally tragic. One has not.

I understand this fascination, and I assume that I would be similarly fascinated. When we see the outcome of disaster, its enormity is somehow ameliorated or abated by the details—the facts that take us from the personal to the generalizable, the qualitative to the quantitative, the unwieldy to the manageable. We relish in the details—the innate detectives and problem-solvers in all of us that crave the information that explains the injustice. We make sense of tragedy by focusing on the pixels, not the picture, as sometimes the picture is too difficult to look at or beyond the limits of our visual field to fully interpret. But it's not only that. The details simultaneously bring us closer together and make us buffered by distance. The details give us a human connectivity made unrelatable by their inimitability. "Sure, anyone can be hit by a car, but in this way, under these circumstances, from this particular angle, with the light diffused just like that, the odds are quite unlikely."

Being hit by a car, irrespective of the outcome, is an identity-transforming event. Immediately, it becomes part of who you are—"I am someone who was hit by a car"—sort of like someone who has been knighted or has witnessed a bank robbery. The event is immediately internalized into how you understand yourself and your relationship to the world. In a frustrating, yet at the same time merciful act of fate or neuroscience, I remember extraordinarily little, if anything at all, of the details of my accident, or even the hours leading up to it. Aside from what family and friends have told me about what took place on the day of my accident, it's almost as if I went to bed on Monday, September 3, 1990, and awoke days later in Stony Brook University Hospital.

I don't remember the precise moment I woke up. The more I think about it, the more I suspect it was an evolutionary waking-up process—isolated moments of consciousness followed by a surrender back into an anesthetic nothingness. So, my awareness of quadriplegia and ventilator-dependence was equally as evolutionary, yet nevertheless revolutionary because every part of my being was revolting against a physical reality I could not comprehend and did not want to believe. Just hours before, my life was as it always had been. I could still feel the warmth of the early-September sunshine on my back, the color of my dark brown hair absorbing all the light it could. I could still run across the baseball fields just adjacent to the highway, hearing the nearby traffic making its presence known. I was not ready. I was not ready to understand my life differently than that. But life-altering events don't always come with announcements. Quadriplegia never provides a warning.

At some indistinguishable number of days after my accident, I remember opening my eyes to a world on its side, existing only within the confines of an indiscriminate spatial field within an anesthetic room. For what I imagine was a long time before I regained consciousness, I had been gnawing on the traumatized area of my tongue, pulling on the stitches with my teeth. I had been fighting the ventilator that was breathing for me, resisting the air that was being forced into my lungs. I had become addicted to and then subsequently weaned off morphine, administered to me to reduce the unfathomable amounts of pain that my body was subjected to. And I know I was trying to pull my mind into some semblance of clarity and consciousness despite the tentacles of injury and oblivion that were wrapped around me. All of these were well in place long before I opened my eyes.

The six weeks I spent in pediatric intensive care were fantastical in the way that an unexpected relocation to Mordor might be fantastical. As a child, Stony Brook University Hospital was, to me, a distant monolith. Though it overlooks the Stony Brook community like the tower of a panopticon, it was always too far to touch, too intimidating to comprehend. A hospital crystallizes so many childhood fears that you are almost forced to avert your gaze, lest the boundaries of your imagination bleed into reality. What is imagined from the outside is only really rivaled by what is experienced on the inside.

There was a time when hospitals were places where people went to die. Before the advent of antibiotics or the use of anesthesia in surgery, hospitals were for the commoner, the marginalized. The hospital was a place where those who were sick would live out their remaining days quarantined from the rest of society. However, when antibiotics became more broadly adopted and after the development of medical licensure and standards of practice, physicians could more safely and reliably perform medical feats previously unimagined. Hospitals, then, became places where people went to get well, not to die, but the public relations campaign has not adapted nearly as quickly as the operational role. The role that the hospital plays in the delivery of care and the saving of lives is immeasurable and unparalleled, that's beyond question. Yet, that fact in no way lessens the fear, anxiety, and vulnerability that come from residing there. After living for six weeks in pediatric intensive care, fear, anxiety, and vulnerability were as familiar as my doctors' faces. They became my strange hospital bedfellows.

My memories are extraordinarily vivid of when I was lying in the pediatric intensive care unit of Stony Brook University Hospital, clinging to life and desperate for answers. My parents, Jean and Ed, and their dearest friends—Jackie and John Macedonia; Mary and Dennis O'Connor—sat vigil by my bedside, day in and day out, looking for any sign of recovery and learning medical jargon and procedures they never desired to learn. At the age of thirty-nine—astonishingly young and almost childlike to be absorbing this enormity, yet at the same time too old to be embarking on a new profession—my parents were thrust into a world whose language they did not understand and whose cultural symbols were foreign. They had to learn how an Ambu bag could be used as a manual resuscitator that, through the power of their hands, could breathe for their daughter. They had to learn what a suction catheter was and how it could alleviate congestion in my lungs to prevent pneumonia. They had to learn that a body paralyzed from its neck down can't regulate autonomic responses like temperature or blood pressure, and how both of these could skyrocket or plummet almost without warning. And they had to learn how to accept a "no change" prognosis; they had to learn how to intellectually interpret words like "incurable," "untreatable," and "permanent" when every fiber in the parental body rejects those words and ideas.

It was a rare and understandably brief privilege during the six weeks I spent in intensive care to visit with my sister, brother, or closest friends. The pediatric intensive care unit was designed for the care of children but not at all for the visitation of children. I don't know what I looked like from the outside, but I suspect it rivaled any child's most horrifying nightmare. I remember when my sister, Kysten, and my brother, Reed, came to see me in the hospital. I cannot, though, envision what a terrifying experience that must have been for them, what a terrifying image to have seen in such a terrifying place. I know that, in that instant, their childhood—not just their childhood as they knew it but, indeed, their entire childhood—was gone. There are sites you see and experiences you undergo that obliterate the innocence that defines childhood. My sister and brother were robbed of theirs, were forced to see a site they could never remove from their minds' eyes, and were dropped, compassless, in the world of adulthood, uprooted from anything that made sense, nomads in a land to which they did not belong. I remember, in and out of states of consciousness, longing for them—longing to be side by side with Kysten in our bedroom. I remember longing to be playing with Reed, toys and games strewn on the den floor, which doubled as molten lava. They were essential pieces of the ballast I needed, they were the levels that could help stabilize the world that had been turned on its side.

In the hospital, even the most mundane aspects of daily life can seem either monumental or in some way off-kilter. The first time I got my hair

washed after my accident was a recovery milestone couched in devastation. I lay in my hospital bed, as that was the only place I could be, and the
PICU nurses and my mother used an aggressively hospital-like golden-
yellow basin and pitcher to pour water over my head. The dirt, pebbles,
blood, and clumps of hair that pooled in the basin made the water look
like the remnants of a puddle on a Civil War battlefield—horrifying but
necessary for me to remove the immediately visible evidence of the scene
of the accident.

The human body is, at once, frighteningly fragile and resolutely resilient. Our bodies break in ways that our spirit can remain unbroken. One
is not the inevitable continuation of the other. We view our personhood
in terms of our bodies. We understand one another by our appearance
and by the physical aspects of being—we can identify a person coming
down the hall by his gait, we can pick up the telephone and know who
we are talking to by the sound of a voice. That is how we understand each
other—that is how we understand ourselves—but that's not who we really
are. When any of those things is lost, damaged, broken, or no longer
recognizable, it is easy to fear that some fundamental part of ourselves is
likewise lost, damaged, broken, or no longer recognizable. The first words
I uttered after my accident were nearly six weeks later, when I was in rehabilitation in New Jersey after leaving Stony Brook. Then and to this day,
my voice is different than it ever had been before. It is breathy and raspy
and subject to modulation that I'm sometimes unable to control. My
voice is different—and something I was, for quite some time, ashamed
of—until I realized that my voice is no more a reflection of my thoughts
than a milk container defines the shape of milk. We place so much of our
identities in our voices, but my voice was not who I was; my ideas and
thoughts were. In the same way, my body was broken in immeasurable
ways, but my spirit and soul and all the ways I was who I was remained

unbroken—committed to survival, committed to reentering the world, and committed to relegating pain and injury to the least impactful role they could play in my life.

But a determined spirit cannot entirely obviate the fragility of the human body, nor can it always fortify tenuous physical circumstances. Neither my family nor I, nor any of the physicians treating me, had any idea whether I would make it from one day to the next, let alone how my life would evolve. For anyone, especially an eleven-year-old, the hospital is an immensely terrifying place—filled with foreign sounds, unfamiliar people, and a reality based on a sense of loss. In my hospital room, IV poles holding bags of blood and liquids took the place of my bedposts. Get-well cards hung on the walls where posters should have been. I could not talk, couldn't eat, couldn't see the world around me, and everything was different. When a person or family is forced to make a hospital a home for any length of time, the notion of normality is completely upended, and you enter an existence characterized by uncertainty and fear, clinging to anything that feels normal or provides peace.

It takes a remarkably short amount of time until being in the hospital infiltrates and attempts to modify the way you understand both yourself and the world. The hospital is simultaneously and bafflingly an atmosphere of overstimulation and sensory deprivation. There is a near continuous din of overly mechanized alarms that either go off for no discernible reason or are so deeply embedded into the hospital culture that they are no longer acknowledged. The fluorescent lights, which seem to know no off function, reflect off the sterilized white walls as if the color white was chosen purely for its reflective properties. The halls and rooms permeate with the smell of biological waste trying to overcome the antiseptic used to mask or detoxify it. And there is a progression of nurses, nurses aides, orderlies, therapists, and visitors so continuous and so regularly paced, it seems they're on a conveyor belt or airport tram. The stimuli are constant and all-consuming, as if to distract you from the reason you're there in the first place.

But at the same time, when you live in the hospital, your senses become oddly dulled, disoriented as to your location in space and time. The hospital is your world, as if nothing exists around it, and your identity is the patient, dependent on benefactors for even the most basic things. It is cocoon-like. It can sometimes be infantilizing. And it disorients you from the world around you and reorients you to a state of near subservience or submission. Almost as if it enters through the IVs or syringes, the presence of the hospital gets inside of you, deep under your skin and into your bloodstream. You become a part of the place and it becomes a part of you: the patient, by definition and by identity.

If these ideas are true for the hospital in an acute setting, they are ever more so in a rehabilitation or long-term care facility, where it's far less treatment with the objective of recovery and release than it is treatment or maintenance for the duration. After spending six weeks in pediatric intensive care in Stony Brook University Hospital, my family and I were told that I had to be moved to a rehabilitation hospital, where I could learn to live my life as a person with a disability. There was no direct route from pediatric intensive care to home; it was a path only traversable by way of rehabilitation hospital—by way of New Jersey.

It took a month and a half following my accident to determine whether I would live and, after that, whether my condition was medically stable enough for me to be moved from the pediatric intensive care unit that had become my home. In order for that determination to be made, the stability of my medical circumstances, in part, had to be engineered with a halo brace. The damage to my cervical spine—my broken neck—put my very survival at risk. For the weeks immediately following the accident, my neck was stabilized in a foam cervical collar—the kind you see worn by characters in movies when they're trying to feign severe injury—but this collar was not strong or protective enough to prevent additional injury in my transport to rehabilitation. We needed something more rigid and immobilizing until my neck could be surgically stabilized, and the halo brace was the next best option.

A halo brace looks like a medieval torture device, a corporal punishment used for only the most heinous of crimes. A description of what a halo brace, in fact, is, does little to change that image. To prevent additional damage to my spinal cord, my head and neck had to be completely immobilized. A halo brace provides that immobility in the most gut-churning of ways: by screwing a metal ring into your skull.

As the name implies, a halo brace looks like a halo—a metal ring that circumscribes a patient's head, about three inches away from the skull at all points. This ring does its job of immobilizing the head through four screws that are drilled into the patient's skull and then, from there, the metal ring is attached to four bars, one at each of the four corners of the skull, each of which is attached to a plastic jacket that the patient wears. It's like a harness, but it prevents the wearer from moving in any direction.

The halo brace was put on me as one of the last agenda items before I could be moved to rehabilitation. It was a procedure done in the hospital operating room, under anesthesia, because it could be so grotesque and certainly so disconcerting.

I can't say for sure if this is an actual memory or a false one that I've constructed over time, but I remember being in the operating room when the halo brace was being put on me. I remember waking up midway through the procedure, when the screw on the right side of my forehead was being drilled into my skull. I remember the terror interlaced with fascination that such a procedure was actually taking place, that I was actually a part of it, and that my encasement in this contraption was the Charybdis I needed to circumnavigate in order to complete my recovery.

I'm not a parent, and I likely will never be one, so I can only understand by proxy how it feels to be a parent looking at her daughter, lying in a hospital bed. With few exceptions, parents view their primary responsibilities in life to include keeping their children protected, safe, and healthy. The instinct is primal—it has to be—traced throughout evolution. There aren't many visions that are more antithetical to this instinct than parents seeing their child—no matter how old or young—in a hospital bed, draped in a hospital gown, with eyes reflecting fear, or eyes not open at all. The parental protective instinct is stunted by an incapacity to ease pain, reverse a diagnosis, or undo an injury. You sit by your child's bedside, and you watch. And you wipe away your intermittent tears of exasperation and pain. You hold your child's hand, rub your thumb along the contour of a knuckle, and ask without expectation of an answer, "Why not me?" This was my parents' life for six agonizing weeks.

The one and only time my parents left my bedside during the six weeks I spent in intensive care was a day in early October 1990, when they had to visit and evaluate potential rehabilitation centers for me to be transferred to after I was released from Stony Brook University Hospital. I was a child and was dependent on medical technology to survive, and these two facts working in tandem reduced the number of facilities that were willing to accept me as a patient to no more than a handful.

Over the course of one anxiety-infused and agony-inducing day, my parents visited all rehabilitation centers within driving distance that were possible next destinations for me. I was terrified to be without them, and they were terrified to leave me. There was little choice in the matter, though, as there was nothing more that could be done for me at Stony

Brook. I needed to learn to live my life as someone with paralysis, and I couldn't return to a house or community that wasn't prepared for me. Rehabilitation—and a long rehabilitative process, at that—was the only choice, and my parents had to select the best option for me within the small range of options, within that solitary choice.

Sterile, institutional, hospital-like, frightening. These were the words my parents used to describe many of the facilities they visited. "There's no way I can allow my daughter to live here," my mother said of one of the facilities they visited. "Children were just propped up in their wheelchairs in front of the nurses' station, staring into oblivion." I'm certain this was the case, and I surely have seen replicas of that image time and time again over the years—the vacancy in people's eyes, limbs contorted not by nature but by negligence, the unbridgeable chasm between those who provide care and those who receive it, the triumph of medical housing over medical home. It is the stuff of nightmares and horror movies—necessary for some, for sure, but desired by nearly none.

By some stroke of luck or fortune, the rehab facility that least reflected these visions also happened to be the one closest to my home. Children's Specialized Hospital in Mountainside, New Jersey, was the last stop that my parents made—a rehabilitation and long-term care facility about two and a half hours away from my home, designed for children with complex medical needs. It was a medical facility—there was no amount of disguise or deception that could cloak that—but the interior spoke more of comfort and familiarity than any standard hospital might. As the town's name would imply, the hospital was built into the side of a mountain, a mansion-like structure that reflected some of the ideas of the deinstitutionalization and community-based care movement of the 1960s. The walls were painted colors—orange, yellow, green—friendly to children and emblematic of a distinct 1970s aesthetic. The campus was wooded, with a long driveway that fed into a pair of double glass doors. It was far from home, yet it was homelike. This hospital would be my home for nearly eight months.

The memories I have of Mountainside are not simply memories but are visions and experiences so deeply embedded in emotion that there is almost a tangibility to them. There was not one single night that I spent at the rehabilitation center when I was not terrified, and there was not a single day when I did not feel like part of my heart was missing, but to say that the time I spent there was categorically gut-wrenching would be to dismiss something far deeper and far more complex.

It would be in rehabilitation that I would learn to live my life again. I would learn how to talk and modulate my speaking in accordance with my breathing through the ventilator. I would learn to sit up again, to view the world from a vantage point not quite vertical but no longer horizontal. I would learn to drive a wheelchair using my mouth, as well as how easily large amounts of paint chip off of walls when scuffed. I would learn how to learn differently, using mental representations in my head rather than what could be worked out on paper. I would learn that in order to get what I wanted and needed in the world, I would have to use my voice and use it effectively, without fear or hesitation. I would come to understand that privacy and dignity mean entirely different things in the hospital than they do on the streets, and that parts of your body whose exposure would often be considered an act of indecency can become commonplace and fair game. I would learn that, even at the age of twelve, you can be considered an adult and—for better or for worse—people will treat you as such. I would learn that social hierarchies can establish themselves in even the most unlikely places, among the most unlikely individuals, and that one's position in a social hierarchy is relative in the same way that relative inequality reflects where we are in our communities, not where we are in the world. I would learn that some of the most pristine and honest pieces of wisdom can come from someone with severe brain damage and, by the same token, some of the most astounding ignorance can come from people with more letters after their names than in them. I would learn that almost anyplace can start to feel like home if you spend enough time there and that people can start to feel like family when enough intimate experiences have been shared. I would learn that there is no limit to the depths at which one can miss another and that this awareness is most acute somewhere between midnight and 2:00 a.m. I would learn that human dignity is an evolving concept, and what might seem like dignity at one point in time can bear no relevance to what does at another point in time. I would learn that the experience of time is doubled when you are longing to be somewhere else. And I would learn that I am much stronger, braver, more adaptable, more patient, and more resilient than I ever could have imagined myself to be.

I shared my hospital room with three other girls, the precise constellation of which would evolve over the seven and a half months that I was a patient there. In an odd way that was only recently made obvious to me by looking retrospectively at that time, our existence at the rehabilitation center was not wholly unlike that of roommates in a college dorm; in fact, even after having spent four years in an actual dorm and two years on top of that as a graduate student living on a university campus, my seven and a half months in rehabilitation was maybe the closest I have had to a true dorm experience.

Rehabilitation life is a unique but highly orchestrated life. Each week, patients would receive a schedule of daily therapies and schooling—our Monday through Friday agenda, roles, and responsibilities that existed as our right to occupancy. Admittedly, there was little in the way of variation from week to week, but these schedules gave the week structure, like these agenda items were our tasks: our work to be done, the payment for which would take the form of one incremental step closer to release from the hospital. Each morning, our own designated primary care nurse would begin the personal care required to get us ready for the day: getting dressed, tending to personal hygiene, suctioning for those of us who needed to have their airways cleaned out, breathing treatments for those whose lungs at some point had failed them, the donning of protective helmets for those whose brains had been injured and traumatized. It was assembly-line style—the rote and almost mechanized approach to work adopted by those who either have too much work to complete in a day or whose work is so personal and so intimate that the only way to survive it is to sterilize it.

Like stockbrokers on Wall Street or lawyers headed into negotiations, by 9:00 a.m. each weekday, we would all be well on our way to the first appointment of the day—physical therapy, speech therapy, occupational therapy, "school," or adaptive aquatics therapy. In thirty- or sixty-minute blocks, that was the objective of the day: Use these media to prepare yourself to enter a world entirely unsuited for and unfamiliar with you. Use these modalities and lessons to learn to live a life that is beyond the realm of what can be taught—learn to do and learn to be in ways you have never done or been before. This was the great fallacy of rehabilitation, the hidden truth of which no one spoke: You can be given tools to live your life, but these tools never come with materials or instructions for assembly. Those must be found on one's own, because the truth of the matter is that until you live with a disability or injury, there is absolutely no way of fully understanding their impact and enormity.

In the years since I was in rehabilitation, I have never spoken to any of the children who were there with me. We were close in a forced way—coming from vastly different backgrounds and experiences, arriving at a common institution for an array of different reasons with none resembling any other—but there was a thread that united us. We were all bound by the experience of a life gone awry, a deviation from plans that we were all forced to accommodate, and an innocence taken too soon.

I remember, quite vividly, a conversation I had with one of the girls who was in the hospital with me. She arrived at Children's Specialized Hospital about one month after I did, or at least that's what it felt like, and before she arrived, I remember hushed conversations among members of the nursing staff that she was going to be tough, someone to be avoided. This was so much the case, in fact, that she was going to be placed in a private room where her "negative influence" would not affect anyone. She was nine years old, from the streets of Newark, at a time when being from Newark implied, however unfairly, something different than it does today, and she had sustained a spinal cord injury from having been shot in the back by a family member. She became my closest friend at the rehabilitation hospital, each of us looking out for the other in different ways. I can only understand now how much she was prejudged and treated with disdain because of social structures that were deeply embedded in how people viewed those different from themselves. She knew this but I didn't, and she was unjustly stronger for it—a strength she would assuredly need to understand and accept her life. But I remember her asking me one night when I was in bed and she was sitting alongside me in her wheelchair, in a moment of uncharacteristically visible vulnerability, "How do we do this? How do we live this life, live like this, forever?" Only twelve years old, I didn't know how to answer that question or even how to incorporate its meaning into my existence. I remember thinking that we had no other choice but to learn to, but I know now that she really meant something deeper than just the day-to-day mundanity of life. I know now that she meant how do you foster the will and fortitude to keep going, especially in a world that will tell you that you can't or you shouldn't or that you don't belong or that there's something wrong with you. I know now that she meant how do you take on each day when you are already taking on so much? At only nine years old, she was far wiser than I was at twelve, and far wiser than most people I have met in all my travels since. She knew what she was up against, as she had already been up against it in other contexts throughout her life.

I don't know what happened to her after she was released from the hospital. I knew she was going to be returning to a high-rise apartment building in Newark that I assume could accommodate her needs only minimally, if at all. I knew that she would be returning to a fractured support system, and to a community that had been allowed to falter due to societal disregard or lack of political concern. I knew she would have to be far tougher than she had ever been before. I can only guess where she might be today, but I have my suspicions that she is nowhere to be seen. It is my hope, though, that the world treated her with more kindness than I expect it had and that she had someone to shape her life as much as she shaped mine.

Many of the children at the rehabilitation hospital received visitors only rarely, if ever. Given the socioeconomic circumstances of many of their families, I understand why. For many of them, parents had to work, and in many cases, there was only one parent to do the working. For others, the distance from home to the hospital was simply too long, making visits on a regular basis too demanding or nearly impossible. And for others, for certain, it was simply easier to not visit—easier physically and easier emotionally. It is easier to put those things of which we hope not to be reminded, like our individual vulnerability or the unsightliness of an injury that has no immediate remedy, out of our sight and, thereby, out of our minds. I can't place judgment on those actions, but I know how immeasurably critical it was for me that my mother stayed with me in New Jersey while I was in rehabilitation.

After Kysten, Reed, and I were born, my mother left her job and stayed at home to raise us. As we got older, she went back to college to complete her degree in teaching and special education, with the goal of working with students with emotional disabilities. That was her dream— to help the most marginalized kids to learn and to thrive. That was also a dream for my family—to have all three children settled in school, with both parents working during the day to pay for life on Long Island, which does not come cheaply, and possibly with some money to spare for the future.

September 4, 1990, was my mother's first day as a full-time teacher of children with emotional disabilities at a local school for children with needs that, in 1990, could not be accommodated in a mainstream class-room. September 4, 1990, was also my mother's last day as a full-time teacher of children with emotional disabilities. From that day forth, the very same day that quadriplegia became part of my family's vernacular, my mother has been by my side, irrespective of distance from home.

It was difficult on my family, but a decision that my parents felt was the right one to make. My mother traveled with me to Mountainside, New Jersey, in the ambulance that provided the only feasible means of transportation. And with the exception of a few sporadic weeks when my father was able to take time away from his work at the Social Security Administration, my mother stayed with me for the more than seven months I was in rehabilitation. She was a comfort to many children there, a maternal presence who did not come in a nurse's uniform or with a stethoscope around her neck. In this informal yet almost naturally predisposing role, my mother was not a caretaker, but the provider of comfort in ways that only mothers serving in the role can provide comfort. She listened to what the children had to say, tied their shoelaces when they needed to be tied, gave them a hug when a hug was far superior to any medication that could be administered. This is what so many children needed. This was, I know, what I needed.

It would be easy to expect that my time in the hospital was a time of devastation and disruption. I would be dishonest if I were to say otherwise—how could it be anything other than that? But that image also isn't a particularly fair one, or at least not a complete one. Unquestionably, spending a total of nine months in a hospital is inordinate, almost too much to imagine for an eleven-year-old. But, perhaps because of its uniqueness and its extraction from the normality of childhood, those nine months are also a bit pristine. It would be almost thirty years later that my brother, Reed, would, by mere happenstance, visit the campus of Children's Specialized Hospital once again, and he told me about the complex emotions he had when he returned. He, too, didn't feel regret or fear or have memories shrouded in sadness. Much like I had, my brother saw that period as a time of difficulty but also one of reference and reverence, one that would change the course of our lives completely. In those nine months, a bond was forged between members of my family and me; we underwent an experience that few others ever undergo and emerged on the other side, maybe not stronger, but certainly intact—certainly more appreciative of each other and unquestionably more aware of the fragility of our lives.

But I learned much more in that time. I learned what it means to love someone and be willing to sacrifice the things you think are important for the sake of protecting those you love. Each weekend, every Saturday morning, my father, brother, and sometimes my sister would come to visit my mother and me in New Jersey. It was the anticipation of that occurrence, that weekly family reunion, that would keep both my mother and me motivated and hopeful throughout the course of the week. While childhood is so often characterized by rivalry among siblings, my sister, brother, and I were forced into a different reality: an obvious disequilibrium that we all shared but that affected us in different ways. We existed in a unique universe, normalized by its abnormality. It was closeness by virtue of distance. There were nights when I would stay awake until sunrise, thinking about what my brother, sister, father, and friends were doing. I would think about what life was like on the other side of the hospital doors—if my friends were thinking about me as much as I was thinking about them, if I could play games with my brother like we had nearly every night before my accident, if my sister and I would ever share a bedroom again. I would also think about whether I would ever actually be released from the hospital and what my life would be like if and when I was. There was a lot of time to think and a lot of ways I could spend time in my head.

I spent a total of nine months in the hospital, enough time to complete a full-term pregnancy and give birth. In some ways, I see this period of time as the very gestation period for my next life—my life as a person with a disability. In a perverse twist of fate, though, of all the things you learn in rehabilitation—all of the mechanics, all the new vantage points, all the ways you never knew humans sometimes had to engage with the world—of all these things, they never teach you—indeed, couldn't teach you—how to be disabled. How to do this. How to live like this, live like this forever. That lesson can only be learned in the doing and the living and in the understandings you gain each day. That lesson is perhaps the most difficult one I have ever attempted to learn, and it has taken me years to learn it. That lesson is a solo mission.

Brooke, graduating with her PhD from Stony Brook University, May 2012.

2

←———→

MECHANICS

You learn that the world that was never designed for
your existence can be changed,
or at least rethought. . . .

I WAS ELEVEN YEARS OLD when I suffered the injuries that would come to shape my life. I was eleven years old when I experienced what would be the most transformative event in my life. At the time, I didn't consider myself particularly young—more of a soon-to-be adult than a child. From my current vantage point, I understand much more realistically how young I was.

Until that point in my life, the phrase "spinal cord injury" was a completely foreign one to me. I had seen people in wheelchairs, and I knew what "paralysis" meant, but I don't think I had a full sense of the mechanics. How could an injury create such long-lasting damage, and in such a strange way? How is it evolutionarily possible that our ability to move and perform the tasks required for life are dictated by such a fragile system that, for all intents and purposes, is unable to repair itself?

Every spinal cord injury is different; each involves the death of a unique constellation of cells and cell types, which affects outcomes in a specific way. Because of the idiosyncratic nature of spinal cord injury, I can claim expertise on my own, but not everyone's. There are undeniable similarities and experiences that unite many people with spinal cord injuries, but just like members of any demographic group, the variation is broad, and it is the nuance of these variations that is most interesting.

WHAT DOES IT FEEL LIKE TO NOT FEEL?

That is a question that I know many wonder but none ever feel they can ask. Other people who live with paralysis may, for sure, have an entirely different experience, but for me, paralysis feels like what it feels like when you are sitting on a park bench or wooden chair and someone is tapping on the wood on the other side—you can vaguely sense that something is happening, you can feel the vibration and pressure, but there is no specificity to it, and you possibly would not even know it was happening, were it not for other cues.

That is what I perceive when I can't perceive a sense of touch, but it is not like my body is dead or not there, much to the contrary, in fact. Though I can't feel to the touch on the outside of my body, I feel with heightened acuity on the inside—every bit of congestion, every cramp or hunger pang. I can feel air entering and leaving my lungs, I can feel when my blood pressure is elevated or low. I can feel when my body is experiencing bone-chilling cold or uncontrollable heat. These are the complexities of spinal cord injury—the inconsistencies that make it such a baffling condition, and one that is so difficult to fully assess. The lengths that physicians went to when trying to determine exactly what my own unique version of paralysis might look like were frustratingly intricate yet ineffectual. Immediately after my accident, while I was still in intensive care, a neurologist would come to my hospital room each day and prick my foot—or at least that is what I imagine he was doing—asking repeatedly, "Can you feel this?" I couldn't, but at the age of eleven, I didn't know how to respond. I didn't know what it meant if I were to say no. I thought that "no" was the wrong answer and that giving that answer would not only mean that I was wrong, but deliberately so—as if I weren't trying hard enough—and perhaps even permanently so. And there was nothing I could do about it. There were times when I would close my eyes, clench my teeth, and concentrate as hard as I possibly could to detect something, the slightest sensation that would indicate that things might be restored or that I was physiologically "right." I remember answering, on more than one occasion, "I think so" or "maybe a little," hoping that the suggestion might prove powerful or translational. As of yet, it hasn't.

For me, inability to describe what paralysis feels like once was less a function of sensory experience than it was a function of emotional understanding. It is one thing to simply know that paralysis makes you unable to feel or to move, but it requires an entirely different degree of introspection and self-awareness to begin to interpret what these inabilities mean and how they become integrated into your life. The challenges faced by people with disabilities like mine, whether congenital or experienced later in life, are real and significant. To deny this would be disingenuous and a glorification not only of disability but also of life, generally speaking. When, like mine, a disability is the result of a life-altering event, the psychological and emotional adjustment from a life as it had been known to a new way of living is nearly unimaginable—and it is because it is so unimaginable that it is so often depicted incorrectly. But if asked with compassion and sincerity, people with disabilities can tell you what their lives are like, what the uniqueness of their circumstances can offer. But they have to be included in the conversation in order for the questions to be asked. As a person with quadriplegia, this is what my life is like—the under-the-covers reality of quadriplegia, ventilator-dependent quadriplegia:

It is an act of existential futility to try to separate our identities from our bodies. I am Italian, and I've often heard it said that "the fastest way to get an Italian to stop talking is to tie their hands behind their backs." What can be said of Italians can really be said for people, in general, irrespective of nationality. We communicate through our bodies; we show affection and express rejection through our bodies; we learn to both understand and navigate the world through our bodies. When living with quadriplegia, the intimacy of the relationship that one has with one's own body is modified, not necessarily in a way that is inferior to most others, but certainly in a way that is different. For instance, I am keenly aware of every regulated breath I take. The delivery and pace of each of the fourteen breaths that enters my lungs every minute are present in my consciousness, so much so that if a breath is delayed by even the smallest fraction of a second, I can tell that there is a problem. I can predict my blood pressure, almost to the precise systolic and diastolic measures, and the concentration of so much tactile sensory information into a small area makes stimulation of my face that much more heightened.

As someone with quadriplegia, "being disabled" encompasses an astonishingly large amount of my day. Quadriplegia forces me to undergo the same personal aspects of daily life that everyone else does, but with help to do it. At first, following my accident, the help I required to do even the most personal things seemed demeaning and beyond the boundaries of polite conversation until I realized that it isn't any more awkward or unspeakable for me than it is for anyone else. My lungs need to be cleared out every few hours to prevent pneumonia. I need to have my body moved around and repositioned throughout the day to prevent pressure sores and blood clots. I abide by the same universal human principle that "everybody poops," which complicates my day in the same way it does anyone else's. But these are all just mechanics. These are all the basic and relatively uninteresting nuts and bolts of life that I'm often asked about, yet they don't really reveal much about quadriplegia and don't amount to much more than peeking into someone's medicine cabinet. This is disability as prepubescent joke telling or voyeurism, and it can be imagined with little more than the most modest degree of creativity. There are many things that are interesting about somebody who experiences quadriplegia, but these are not them. What's truly interesting is what lies in the depth of their experience, the creativity it requires to adapt to every task they undertake, and their willingness to take on challenges every day.

BEING PATIENT AND BEING CREATIVE

I have come to see quadriplegia as not just a diagnosis, but as a prescribed way of life with unusual ways of doing things that we all have to do by virtue of our humanity. Quadriplegia is, if nothing else, a demonstration of a human being's depth of patience. When you live with quadriplegia, much of life is lived with the assistance of someone else or experienced by proxy through someone else. Unless it is possible to engineer it differently, it can sometimes seem like the world exists just beyond reach or like you are not entirely a member of it. This fact might be more intuitively evident than some of the more nuanced aspects of daily life as a person with quadriplegia. It is hard to fully appreciate how much of our daily activity is automatic or reflexive until that level of automation or reflexivity is no longer there. When you live with quadriplegia, the physical might not be controlled by the subconscious, but it is very much affected by it. The inclination to turn toward the source of an unexpected sound or the contraction of muscles when you're startled take place in the mind but are not executed by the body. The emotions that underlie these evolutionarily reflexive actions just sit on you like weights, like unresolved anxiety.

But you learn to be patient, to wait for things that few others ever have to wait for, like the scratch of an itch, the brushing away of a stray lock of hair from your face, or the next mouthful of dinner after you have swallowed the mouthful before. You have to wait for someone to help move an object that obscures your field of vision; you have to wait for someone to open the door to exit your house or even your very own bedroom; you have to wait to live much of your life until there is someone willing and able to help you live it. And all of this requires patience. Infinite patience the likes of which can sometimes feel beyond the parameters of human ability. It is an act of necessity driven by abnormality. It is fundamentally unnatural-feeling to ask for help doing the most mundane but personal tasks. It requires an odd combination of self-confidence and humility to empower the strength to be reliant, and it doesn't come easily. So, you wait. You wait until the right person presents herself at the right time, and in so doing, you test the depths of the human capacity to be patient. And you do this all day, day in and day out.

But there is an intensity of focus that is almost a necessary antecedent to patience. Living with quadriplegia, time passes at no slower nor more rapid a pace than it does for anyone else, yet the moments are somehow richer—an expansion of depth rather than length. I perhaps tire more easily due to quadriplegia, but I also tire less easily; I can stare into a computer screen from early morning to late evening without noticeable fatigue and, by mere demands of circumstance, have sought ways to circumvent the barriers that might stymie those who would ordinarily not encounter them.

How do you read a book when you can't turn the pages? How do you write a dissertation when you can't touch the keyboard? How do you live your life as a fully autonomous adult when, by virtue of physical circumstance, the cloak of dependence lies over all that you do? And how do you get people to listen and pay attention when listening and paying attention can seem beyond the courtesies they ought to afford you? Attempting to solve even one of these would be enough to test anyone's deepest reserves of resilience. And it does. But you learn to pursue them anyway. Through repetition, you learn that the world that was never designed for your existence can be changed, or at least rethought, when enough attention has been shifted away from the intractability of the problem to the possibilities of its solution.

Patience and creativity, especially when you live with a disability, are inseparable concepts. For people who face quadriplegia, every day is a test of creativity, a forced opportunity to find paths around the inevitable obstacles that present themselves with both unexpected and expected regularity. As you live longer into the years of quadriplegia, these challenges, surprisingly, do not reduce in number or extremity, you just become more adept at handling them. The tools you have at your disposal become sharpened and more ready for use, and your sense of resilience becomes stronger in your efforts to overcome them. There is a life to be lived that will not wait for solutions to present themselves—a life that involves places to see, a life that involves unexpected mechanical failures that need to be addressed, a life that involves relationships that wait to be developed—and you learn to become a part of the intended outcome.

TECHNOLOGY

For many, technology is the means by which the limitations of human capability are stretched. That is nothing new, and its logic makes perfect sense. The human brain can calculate equations only so quickly; the human body can work only so fast; human vision can see only so far into the distance; and human memory can retain only so much information. Technology, for as long as human beings have used their own brainpower to develop it, has been the very mechanism by which we have augmented our reality and have allowed human beings to exceed their expected potential. Particularly over the past several decades, in which the advancements of technology have been achieved at a literally exponential pace, we are sometimes more android than human, more mechanical than organic. While some have argued that technology is the answer to the question of human limitation, there are few who feel the extent of human physical limitations more than people with disabilities. Yet they are often the ones for whom technology is least available and least accessible.

The marginal benefit that technology has on the lives of people with disabilities is enormous, and this was a fact made known to me so early on after my accident, when I transitioned from intensive care to rehabilitation.

Rehab, for me, was more of a physical location than it was a process: the place where I would learn to live, or become capable, once again. When I was in rehabilitation, one of the very first goals set for me was to restore my ability to engage with the world in ways I had before. First among these was restoring my ability to talk, which seems far less a technology-driven accomplishment than it actually was.

Many who breathe with the assistance of a ventilator are unable to speak at all. The explanation is frustratingly simple: When people typically speak, air in the lungs moves past the vocal cords, causing a reverberation that produces the voice and sound. However, for many people who breathe through a ventilator, air that is in their lungs is not always exhaled in the same way, as it leaves the lungs in the same way it entered it: through a tracheostomy tube surgically inserted in the throat and a circuit of plastic tubing connected to the ventilator. This mechanical system and mechanized way of life can make speech an impossibility for many ventilator users, or at least make their voices soft, irregular, breathy, and strained. When I was in rehabilitation, my first milestone was to regain my ability to communicate, even if that meant in a way and in a sound that was wholly unlike how I understood my voice and speech before. The gift of my voice was restored to me through a piece of technology as simple as it is life altering.

If it's true that people on ventilators have difficulty talking because the air in their lungs escapes through the tube that allows air to enter, it should also be true that a system could be devised to allow air to go in one direction (in) but not the other (out). If that could be engineered, air could be exhaled past the vocal cords, like everyone else. A quadriplegic with muscular dystrophy designed a one-way valve, called the Passy Muir Valve, with that very vision in mind.

Mere days after I arrived in rehabilitation, a small, cylindrical piece of plastic, about an inch in length and even less than that in diameter, was inserted into my ventilator tubing for the first time. It had been seven weeks since my accident. Seven weeks of silence and seven weeks of frustration. While inhaling and exhaling are such evolutionarily intuitive practices, to be taught to do them is jarring and uncomfortable; it forces you to retread parts of development that seem infantile, and you subsequently *feel* infantile. But what my family and I had initially thought would be lost to me forever was restored, and though my voice is staggeringly different than it ever had been when I was a child, it is a shape-shifting, transformative representation of who I am now. My voice is breathy and raspy and forces me to answer the questions "Do you have a cold?" or "What's wrong with your voice?" with regularity, but it's mine. I love it—the ingenuity that makes it possible, the mouth that brings it to life, and the brain that propels it.

As a speech giver, lecturer, and even as a writer, my voice is the vehicle by which I share my life and thoughts with the world, but quadriplegia also severely limits one's ability to interact physically with this world. Immediately after my accident, I feared a life of being bedridden. For a full six weeks while in intensive care, a bedridden existence was my life, looking at the same walls each day, the only variety contingent upon the side of my body I was arbitrarily turned onto. But the wheelchair that has since become indistinguishable from my identity was the technology that changed this.

Quadriplegia precludes the use of wheelchairs as many people understand wheelchairs: relatively small, light, and propelled by one's hands. Quadriplegia demands the utilization of something much weightier and more technological. The wheelchair I used for many years after my accident was driven through the intermittent application of pressures of air puffed into or sipped from a straw. My wheelchair would go in one direction or another based on the amount of pressure applied. While sophisticated in its description, this technology is far from ideal, rudimentary in its design, and frustrating, if not sometimes dangerous, in its use. I was able to abandon this technology for a more sophisticated wheelchair-activation system right before heading to Harvard for college in 1996.

Around that time, as technology advanced for everyone, wheelchair-activation technology for people with quadriplegia made a rare jump. The Tongue Touch Keypad system allowed people with no movement in their arms and legs the ability to control a wheelchair using a remote control that was accessed by the tongue. It looked, for all intents and purposes, like a retainer thickened by anaphylaxis, with a series of nine buttons on the palate that could be pressed by the tongue. This technology was, without understatement, revolutionary for me. Not only did it allow me to activate my wheelchair without the obstruction of a straw in my face, which was the necessary configuration of the sip-and-puff system, it also allowed for the activation of many other environmental controls, like the television, telephone, and, most importantly, the mouse attached to my computer.

In a way that was different from how I had interacted with the world at any point in my life before, this system allowed me to be as independent as I could be. Once someone put the keypad in my mouth, I could move from one room to another without anyone's assistance. I could pull up to my computer and start doing my work. I could pull away from my computer and head into my bedroom, where I could make a phone call or watch television. And I could do all of these things with nearly the same degree of autonomy and ease that anyone else might enjoy. This was the technology that saw me through my years in college, my years in graduate school, and my time on the campaign trail. It was a gift of independence when much of that independence had been taken away.

It is astonishing how quickly we begin to take basic liberties and freedoms in our lives for granted, irrespective of how modest in nature. That's what happened in the years that I used the Tongue Touch Keypad system. I became used to the freedom of moving from one room to another, unassisted, or making a phone call to a friend without an intermediary to accomplish the task. But in January 2011, when I was just beginning my research and writing for my PhD dissertation, I received a telephone call from the owner of the company that had developed the Tongue Touch Keypad. He told me that the product was no longer profitable for him, and as a result, he was closing his business and discontinuing the technology. I had just come home from meeting with my dissertation advisors, had just planned a path forward on my research of stem cell research , and was so eager to begin my work. This phone call and the news it contained was like becoming paralyzed all over again. In an instant, it felt as though I was being, once again, denied the very basic aspects of life that everyone else does not think twice about. It was frightening. It was stagnating. It was paralyzing.

But when you have been paralyzed once, to hell with becoming paralyzed twice. Within a few hours of that phone call, I regained my composure and began calling all of the people who I thought could be helpful in solving this problem. My first call was to my colleague Miriam, at Stony Brook University, whose decades-long career in engineering had brought her into contact with technological and engineering experts of all kinds. Even more, it taught her to view problems from a creative vantage point that is undaunted by obvious obstacles and fixated on solutions.

This is a niche problem, I know, and one born out of luxury, as many people with disabilities fight every day for even the most basic needs and opportunities. But for years now, Miriam and her colleagues have assisted me with technological solutions to complex access challenges. I have had to return to the sip-and-puff wheelchair activation system that I used years ago, but through technological advancements and innovations made by students under her guidance, she has helped ensure that my most significant obstacles could be surmounted. But over the years, it has become even more than that. Working together on various initiatives, we have focused on how the needs created by disability—or, really, human limitation of any kind—are alleviated by how we direct our human brilliance and our resources. Technology is and has always been the mechanism that brings the limits of human capability closer to the actualization of human goals. However, despite the technological world in which we live today, people with disabilities are often left out of technological advancement in the very same way that they are left out of much of life in general. The former is merely a proxy for the latter.

MARGINALIZATION AND EXCLUSION

Technology only brings us so far. There is a logistical divide that technology cannot overcome without social motivation behind it. In fact, there is a hollowness to our technological endeavors without a social imperative of inclusion to support them. There are gaps in society that, irrespective of the brilliance behind our innovation, have still left people behind. It is far too often the case that people with disabilities are merely left out of the conversations we have about the evolution of technology or the construction of public policy or, really, nearly anything else. There are inroads that, no doubt, have been made, but many of these fall under the isolated and rarely visited category of "disability stuff," rather than incorporating disability into already existing conversations about the needs found in human experience. It is disability as a "disability-related" matter rather than disability as a human matter, and that conflict has made it easier for society to exclude people with disabilities.

The marginalization and exclusion of people with disabilities is an issue that I have given a great deal of attention to throughout my life. It is nearly impossible to live with a physical disability and not be aware of the explicit and implicit signals that are sent—some deeply institutionalized and others occurring almost frivolously—that say, without equivocation, that you are not welcome or that your inclusion is an act of charity. These signals have consequences, both of a personal and societal nature. There were many years of my life when I felt that anyone seeking to befriend me was doing me a favor. I intrinsically underestimated my own value in a friendship, failed to measure my own self-worth or what I could contribute to a relationship. As a result, particularly in the years immediately after my accident, there were points in my life when I had fewer friends than I thought I should have had. And I overestimated the value of some of the friendships I did have.

The social exclusion that so many people with disabilities experience is real, and it is painful. And far too often, it feels like it is deserved.

I entered college when I was seventeen years old. It was nearly six years after my accident, but it wasn't until that point in my personal evolution that I was forced to tell my story, to articulate the blueprint of my life, to claim ownership of my own personal narrative in ways I never had before, and to no longer be afraid of it. It was in the process of this storytelling and owning of my identity that I realized I had to relearn myself, to begin to think less like the one who was ensnared by a beast and more like the one who had defanged it. It was in this process that I realized how desperately I needed to rid myself of the limited beliefs I had about my worth and value. I had to reinterpret and ultimately reject my prior acceptance of being unnecessarily excluded from so much of social life, as if being excluded from life and all of its richness is something anyone should ever accept. It took my removal from the comfort and familiarity of my home and family to realize that I also had value and worth beyond that immediate circle. It forced me to see myself as a contributor to conversations that mattered; it forced me to see myself in the way that others saw me and not be afraid of it. And I was proud of what I saw.

For many years now, I have lived with the privileged status of one comfortable in her place in the world and without doubt in terms of the importance of the contributions she can make. I am no longer afraid of myself or of the phrase "disabled woman." However, events over the past several years shook some of those beliefs, forcing me to reevaluate many of the assumptions I had made about how I relate to disability and how disability is valued.

"Inclusion" and "diversity" are hotly discussed topics in social conversation and organizational management and have been for quite some time. In addition to being morally right, the less-altruistic logic behind the movement toward greater diversity and inclusion among all sectors of society is simple: Society is better off, and organizations can work more efficiently, when people of diverse backgrounds are a part of them. Different experiences and diverse opinions expose new realities that would otherwise have been hidden or not fully understood. Organizations and society are much better able to make the changes necessary to meet the demands of a similarly changing world when they can better understand how they sit in relation to everyone. It is of economic sense and a humanitarian imperative that the diverse nature of our world is met with strategies to include everyone in it. While inclusion efforts have been made, and rightfully so, to address some of the social disparities experienced by people of diverse racial and ethnic backgrounds—including increasing representation in the media, better understanding the sociocultural forces that shape diverse lives, and righting a history of legislative wrongs that have systemically disenfranchised, discriminated against, or in some other way disadvantaged people because of their culture, heritage, or other characteristic—many of the same efforts have yet to be made in any meaningful way to benefit people with disabilities. And this fact is true even in some of the most unexpected places.

In 2015, I was an assistant professor at Stony Brook University and had politics deep in the marrow of my bones. It was coming up on the last year of the Obama administration, and I knew I had experiences and knowledge to offer in the field of public policy. After having run for New

York State Senate in 2006, I was not ready to run for public office again. But the experience had fueled my desire to help shape policy, to lend my voice and ideas to how the country would work. At the very beginning of the year, I submitted my name and application to serve as a White House Fellow.

The White House Fellows program was created in the 1960s under the Lyndon Johnson administration and was designed to expose emerging leaders to the intricacies of the policymaking and legislative world. Each year, a class of ten to twenty people from all backgrounds, with a common desire to take part in public service, is chosen from a national candidate pool, and those chosen spend a full year serving in one of the departments of government. The selection process was precisely as onerous and potentially intimidating as one would expect in order to serve in the top tiers of federal government: The initial application required essays on your contribution to government, your thoughts on the value or contribution that government has in public life, and finally an analysis of a policy measure that was in need of modification or introduction. I submitted my name and application, along with letters of recommendation, my résumé, and accounts of personal accomplishments.

My essays described my experiences running for office and how the policies we implement serve as the framework by which people can achieve the lives they want; how public policy is the mechanism by which the future is built both collectively and individually; and how the laws we enact are a representation of our societal priorities and the opportunities we provide each other to create a society we all want to be a part of. These were the ideas that I had spoken about as a candidate for New York State Senate, and these were the ideals that I thought our government needed to talk more freely about. I wrote my policy analysis on stem cell research and strategies that the U.S. could use to broaden its stem cell research policy framework to allow additional avenues of research to be funded by federal research dollars, using this isolated issue as an archetype for our commitment to science research in general. Science, I wrote, was the best and most tangible path toward development and we needed to allow it to advance both progressively and ethically.

In February I received a letter from the White House informing me that I had been chosen as a regional finalist for the fellows program. This next round of the selection process would involve a series of interviews and activities held over two days in New York City, with interviews conducted by current and previous White House Fellows. "Let me just give it a try and see how I do," I said to my parents after getting the letter. "It will just be a couple of days and then I'll forget about it," I said, expressing a conviction that I didn't quite feel in my heart.

On a cold March afternoon, my parents and I drove from Long Island to the Ford Foundation headquarters, where the interviews were scheduled to take place. The first event was a "get to know you" session, followed by a dinner with interviewers. I was nervous but not inordinately nervous—the type of nervous you get when you feel like you *have* to be nervous—and my interactions with the other regional finalists were exactly as I had expected them to be, exactly how my interactions on an isolated basis often are, on the surface and without intimacy. The interviews were to start first thing the next morning, at 8:00 a.m., and would go the whole day, three interviews each on a staggered basis. Many of the regional finalists were from New York City, so after the first night's events, they simply went home, got a good night's sleep, and arrived back at the Ford Foundation the following morning. Given the quick turnaround time from the night's events to the interviews the following day, my parents and I decided that it would be unreasonable and maybe even impossible to get back to Long Island, get into bed—a process that takes nearly two hours—get some sleep, and then wake up and get ready—which can take up to five hours—and be back in New York City by 7:30 the following morning. So the reasonable and sensible thing to do was to find a hotel in New York City and stay there, irrespective of how little sleep we might get.

How even the simplest of plans get foiled. My parents and I pulled up to the hotel, only blocks away from the Ford Foundation, only to find that the hotel was inaccessible. The hotel had touted its "accessibility," but what is described as accessible on paper can be utterly inaccessible in actuality. The Americans With Disabilities Act (ADA), the landmark civil rights legislation for people with disabilities that passed in 1990, had provided the legal guideposts within which I had lived my life as a girl and then a woman with a disability, its passage having taken place only mere months before my accident. Yet the legislation has its limitations: a lack of strong enforcement; a lack of clarity in terms of all it includes versus what people, businesses, and entities would like to believe it includes; and a lack of public support and awareness to demand more for people with disabilities when protections fail to go far enough. I had seen this time and time again, in businesses I would try to frequent, restaurants I would try to patronize, public spaces I would try to access. The ADA has brought to light the ongoing access challenges that people with disabilities face, yet even in its thirty-year history, the legislation accounts for far too few needs, far too little of the time.

With the clock ticking and hours of potential sleep waning, my parents and I made the decision to drive home, pulling into the driveway at 11:00 p.m. I slept in my wheelchair that night rather than take the time to get into bed, tilting my wheelchair back as far as I could to alleviate any pressure on my body from sitting in the chair so long. It was uncomfortable and something I knew none of my fellow regional finalists had to take into account. We were back on the road, headed to New York

City, at 4:00 a.m.—early enough to see a family of deer grazing on the side of the road. The streets of New York were essentially empty when we arrived—they were as lifeless as we were feeling, having gotten virtually no sleep and having spent 70 percent of the previous ten hours on the road. But we made it, even arriving before anyone else. Throughout the course of the day, I had my three interviews, each in front of a team of three interviewers, and then took part in a group exercise. In the group exercise, all the finalists were presented with a group problem—a policy issue we had to address—and each of us was assigned a department of government. We had to devise a policy that this department could introduce to help solve this common problem. Department of government assignments were being passed around, and I thought, "Come on, Department of Health . . . Department of Education would be pretty good too . . . I think I could even make Department of State work." I got my assignment: Department of the Interior. I remember thinking, "Perfect. Just my luck. Nobody knows what the Department of the Interior does."

But I must have done something right, as a week later I was notified that I had been advanced to a White House Fellows national finalist. Each geographic region had picked two national finalists who would all assemble that upcoming June in Washington, D.C., for a three-day retreat of interviews, leadership-building exercises, and group challenges, resulting in the final selection of the White House Fellows.

My parents and I drove down to Washington, D.C., on a Tuesday in June. The previous weekend, my brother, Reed, and his wife, Ellen, had gotten married in Pennsylvania, a ceremony and reception filled with family and friends in which I was a bridesmaid, so by the end of that week, I-95 and my van were extremely well acquainted. In the previous months, I had been in close contact with representatives from the White House Fellows program, talking about how we could best make accommodations for the three-day retreat, thinking through details that I was certain were rarely, if ever, thought through before. We needed to discuss the hotel room I would stay in, one that would be large enough to accommodate my wheelchair and my parents, and how they could coordinate for me to have a height-adjustable "hospital" bed in my room. We needed to identify any particular access accommodations that would have to be made, like where I could go to address medical necessities throughout the course of the three demanding days or even when I would have the opportunity to address them. We had to think about how I could travel from the hotel where the interviews would take place to various outings in D.C., when everyone else would be traveling either by foot or by taxi, and any other specifications they could arrange so that my attendance would be possible. This was new yet important information for the White House staff to learn.

Also over those months between the regional and national finals, I spoke to representatives from the White House Fellows program about accommodations that could be made in the event that I were selected as a fellow. I was not at all presumptuous about the likelihood of that happening, but I wanted to start thinking along those lines in case it did. Could some portion of my service be done in New York? Was there a way that things could be arranged so that my parents would not have to be separated for the full year? Could we find reliable and secure transportation to take me from a home base to work? These were the sorts of questions that my parents and I needed to have addressed if this were to be possible at all, and we addressed them in the same deliberate, methodical way we had addressed many other opportunities and circumstances that had arisen over the years. The orchestration of all these logistical details was new to the White House Fellows program, yet entirely routine for my family and me. There was a lot of work to be done but also a lot of knowledge to offer to individuals deep within political circles who had never encountered any situation like mine before. My participation in the program would be unconventional but not impossible.

The retreat involved two days of interviews, three interviews per day in front of three interviewers per session. The interviewers were not former White House Fellows, as they had been in the regional interviews, but instead were people of significant influence in government, journalism, and culture. The interviews started early in the morning, went straight through the day, and then were followed by social activities of the most unrelaxing sort. It was intellectually intense and extremely rigorous, probably among the most challenging and mentally taxing undertakings I had ever subjected myself to, and also physically taxing in the exact same measure. But it was the very type of exhaustion that I love—exhaustion born out of intense engagement, brought about by thinking about problems and how to address them, predicated on challenging myself to think better and think bigger. After the intense interview retreat concluded, I left Washington and drove home with my equally exhausted parents, thoroughly invigorated.

I had gone down to Washington, D.C., wanting to do my best, to demonstrate to myself and everyone involved in the program that I had something meaningful to offer, something important to say, and that my involvement in the program would signify something of value. I left feeling that I had done just that—that I had spoken about issues of importance to me, answered questions without hesitation, and was fully committed to tackling challenges we faced as a nation.

It was several weeks before I heard anything from the White House Fellows program, and given the length of time, it took very little intellectual effort to deduce the outcome. I had not been chosen to be a White House Fellow. It was a sting that I, quite frankly, was not expecting. However, my first nephew, Carter Edward Sinclair, one of the deepest loves of my life, was born that following September, and had I been chosen for the fellowship, my mother and I would have missed much of the first year of his life, so I have not a single regret about that outcome. Nor do I regret having embarked upon the process to begin with, as I had challenged myself in a way I never had before and came out stronger for it. Nonetheless, I do think an unfortunate decision was made.

I was, through this process, undoubtedly surrounded by some of the most talented, committed, and extraordinary people with whom I could ever hope to associate. That is beyond question. I don't know what factors ultimately went into the decision to not include me on the final list, and I would not ever suggest that the decision was made on unfounded argumentation. Perhaps I did not offer what they were looking for. Perhaps, and quite possibly, the events of my life were not as exceptional or impressive as those of others. But the marginal difference in exceptionality and impressiveness from one individual to another at that level was, and I suspect often is, modest at best. Were there people in that group who were smarter than I was? Of course, and probably much more so. Were there people in the group who had experienced war or service in ways I never have? Without question, and I thank them for their service. But I also know that not one of the chosen White House Fellows had seen the world from my vantage point or had lived a day with disability at its most extreme. Not one of them could fully understand the additional thought and effort that went into my participation as a national finalist, nor how valuable these tools would be to the very kind of problem-solving that people with disabilities incorporate into their lives and future politicians ought to emulate. The prominence of physical struggle was, in many respects, absent from the consideration. In fact, one of the noted activities of the White House Fellows orientation session is a physical challenge, involving climbing and military-based training skills. And that, I believe, is most unfortunate—not for me, but for the program and all who derive something from it.

Just as there was much of value for me to learn through the program, there was also much of value for me to offer. Conversations and ideas begin to look very different when the perspectives of those not often thought of begin to be included. Matters of health policy, education policy, infrastructure, Social Security, and even national security take on different dimensions when the lives of those who engage with these issues differently are acknowledged and then are taken into account.

The truth of the matter is that we can't have any real, complete conversations regarding matters of public policy without also talking about people with disabilities or understanding their perspectives. We can't talk about poverty without also acknowledging that people with disabilities are among the most persistently disadvantaged throughout the world, with nearly 30 percent of people with disabilities living in poverty in the U.S. compared to 13.6 percent of their nondisabled counterparts. We can't talk about health care without also acknowledging that people with disabilities have less access to health-care services and, as a result, experience unmet health-care needs more frequently than any other demographic group. We can't discuss improvements to our education system without also understanding that children with disabilities are more likely than any other vulnerable group to drop out of school, and that these children not only experience barriers to schools themselves, but also experience learning barriers while in the classroom. We can't hope for equal opportunity in employment without also admitting that unemployment for people with disabilities is a chronic problem, creating an enormous economic loss as well as a devastating loss of talent. And we could never mobilize true criminal justice reform without knowing how disproportionately affected people with disabilities are when it comes to arrests, abusive treatment in incarceration, and the use of the death penalty. We *can* talk about these things, but we don't. And we don't because the voices of those who advocate on their behalf might not be seen for the value they hold. That is what was missed. That individuality of experience and richness of potential contribution was lost. That is where the nature of inclusion was miscalculated.

Contrary to what many people believe about its mechanics, quadriplegia is a disability and not an ailment. When you face a disability, the distance that people can keep—physically and emotionally—is as if out of fear of contamination or contagion. This distance and hesitation were things I was expecting to experience after my accident because I was a victim of the very same socialization that we are all indoctrinated into and was subjected to the same sociocultural beliefs about disability—that marginalization and exclusion are what disability brings about and these are what people with disabilities deserve. When you live with a physical disability, the types of sideways glances and averted gazes that would baffle most are simply commonplace. When you live with a physical disability as extensive as mine, you become accustomed to mothers redirecting the chins of children who innocently stare with curiosity. When you live with a physical disability as extensive as mine, you become quite familiar with the extremes of the bipolarity: people who are overly solicitous and feel it is their responsibility to help—which, for all intents and purposes, it is, irrespective of how condescending the offer might be, though it shouldn't be—and the people who would more easily and comfortably not exert the energy to make eye contact. You live within these extremes, which largely average to a sustainable midpoint, but with wild swings in either direction.

I understand the psychology behind this, as well as the sociology behind it. There is an aspect of disability that makes people uncomfortable, and that discomfort becomes apparent in their actions, whether or not they intend it to be. I have given long and hard thought to the psychological and sociological reasons people run away from disability, and while no single explanation encompasses everyone or explains everything, the reasons taken together present a pretty comprehensive picture.

Psychological

For many, disability is synonymous with some form of impairment. Impairment, in turn, seems to signify the abnormal. The vulnerable. The weak. As humans, we rarely choose vulnerability over empowerment or weakness over strength, as vulnerability and weakness are threats to our very survival. We are evolutionarily and biologically predisposed to remove ourselves from threats to our survival, to those things that we perceive to be sources of danger. It is the fight-or-flight response that we all know, all too well—the cascade of hormonal responses initiated by a perception of danger or threat. Disability, then, becomes an aspect of identity that intimidates us and makes us feel at risk. It subjects us to what is called, in psychological terms, amygdala hijack, or an emotional response that is immediate and overwhelming and disproportionate to the actual triggering event or stimulus, causing a fight-or-flight response when such a response is not biologically or psychologically necessary.[2] Whether or not it's done with our overt awareness, we distance ourselves from it just like we would distance ourselves from any other threat.

This might seem like an exaggeration, but the effects are real, and I have felt them many times. Sometimes it's less implicit than others.

After my brother graduated from business school with an MBA and was headed into the world of accounting, my parents and I went apartment hunting with him in the Boston, Cambridge, and Brookline areas of Massachusetts. These geographic areas are not at all known to be seats of backward thinking and are among the most liberal and progressive in the country. We looked at apartments in a building in North Cambridge, a mere mile or two away from where I had spent some of the most meaningful and formative years of my life. We arrived at one of the encircled apartment buildings, and a woman dressed in a long, white, flowing gauzy summer suit watched from a balcony as we entered the building with the real estate agent. This woman, the apparent height of Bohemian progressivism, was waiting for us when we came out of the building. She came up behind me, toward my father, finger pointed and voice raised, and said, "We don't want any of your kind here. This building is not for your kind of people." I was both shocked and devastated, in equal measure. Shocked, because nothing like that had ever been said to me so vehemently or directly. I had considered Cambridge to be my home, the place where I found my voice and sense of self, and this was a harsh violation of that. And I was devastated not simply because of that particular treatment but also because I felt like I was to blame. I felt like the very nature of my existence was enough to complicate the lives of people in my family. I felt as though my life and deeply personal aspects of my identity were sources of ridicule, and I was ashamed.

It was Mark Twain who said, "Repartee is something we think of twenty-four hours too late." And while I—in no way—was eager to engage in repartee with this woman, by the next day, after the initial affront had worn off, I found myself wishing I had said, "You'd better hope this place doesn't start discriminating on the basis of abhorrent behavior because you'll find yourself out of a home" or "Do you mind telling me what 'my kind' is? Because if you walk across Mass Ave. and happen to be hit by a car, then my kind is also your kind." Those were the things that she needed to hear because she was never forced to think about them.

That incident still resonates deeply with me and remains so vividly emblazoned in my mind. It reminds me of the very same experiences that many Black and Brown people underwent—and continue to undergo—as they looked for places to settle with their families and raise their children. While the history and experiences are vastly different, there are strong parallels. The unfortunate inclination is to marginalize and make uncomfortable those of whom we are fearful, those we perceive as a threat, those to whom we feel superior. Disability reminds people of their mortality as human beings, it reminds people that our physical prowess can change at any time, for anyone. That's frightening, and there is no way to deny it. But just because that's the way it often is, there is no good reason to believe that that is the way it ought to be. Much the opposite, in fact. We can learn to manage our fears through exposure. We can even learn to counteract the amygdala hijack. But these take work, they take repetition, and they take an environment that fosters it. What lies in our psychology is significant and influential, but these psychological predispositions have been repeatedly bolstered, reinforced, and exaggerated by what we have embedded in our culture and what we have socialized ourselves into believing.

Sociological

Disability is a regularly occurring aspect of human identity, taking place congenitally, naturally, or due to injury or accident. While disability occurs at about a 15 percent prevalence rate in the general population, we still view it as an anomaly. It makes sense to put this into some perspective. With a global population of a little over 7.8 billion people, there are over 1.1 billion people living with disability around the world. In the United States, with a population of about 331 million, this same percentage equates to almost 49 million people. While many studies and much research has indicated that disability is disproportionately higher in developing countries or countries that have been subjected to years of war and conflict, these estimates are roughly accurate across the globe, and as a result, people with disabilities comprise the largest minority in the world. Yet it is sometimes like a rare anthropological event to spot a person with a disability "in the wild." People see one of the 1.1 billion people with disabilities on the street or in a common building and it is often like they are seeing a vampire or an unmasked superhero. "Whoa, what are you doing here?" "Are you supposed to be here or are you lost?" And this happens in the most commonplace of common places—the store, the bank, a school, a meeting, anywhere other than the hospital or institution that people expect we may have escaped from. It is in the more elite and less frequented circles that things become even more unbalanced. Regrettably, far too few people with disabilities hold visible positions of leadership—whether in politics, business, academia, or any other discipline that affects their lives just as much as it affects anyone else's. There are far too few people with disabilities who are considered to be role models in the true, Mertonian definition of the term: "a person whose behavior, example, or success is or can be emulated by others, especially by younger people."[3] That is to the detriment of everyone, not simply those who are most obviously and immediately affected.

It is much more regularly the case that people with disabilities are shamed and disparaged for their identities rather than recognized for their accomplishments and contributions. The representation of disability in society and culture has reflected this very idea. The cultural depictions of disability, whether on television, in literature, in film, or sometimes in art, follow and reinforce a trope that has long been established for disability, and an uncreative and ill-informed trope, at that. Despite the fact that disability is such a common individual characteristic and identity, it is represented very infrequently in popular culture, and when it is, it is of such gross exaggeration and stereotyped depiction that it is the disability that becomes the identity rather than a part of a complex identity.

Disability Studies is an intellectual discipline that's designed to challenge how disability is viewed, to shift thinking from interpreting disability as an individual defect to understanding it as a product of social, political, cultural, and economic factors. Disability, from this standpoint, isn't a medical problem but a regularly occurring aspect of life. Disability Studies scholars and even organizations like the U.N. have given a great deal of attention to this phenomenon, the misrepresentation of disability in popular culture and its attachment to human characteristics that are unattractive, at best. When there are disabled characters in books, movies, or television shows, they are the "disabled character" rather than a character who happens to have a disability. That is who they are. That is their character. And because disability is the defining feature of disabled characters, their idiosyncrasies, behaviors, maladaptation, foibles, and even mundane experiences somehow become associated with disability rather than with the character herself. Disabled characteristics rather than human characteristics are portrayed because that's what we are taught to pay attention to.

Scholars who spend their lives focusing on these questions have uncovered perplexing and disturbing patterns in how people with disabilities are represented in the media.[4] Disability has been associated with unwellness, unwellness with contagion or infection, and then contagion with something to be rejected or feared. People with disabilities are rarely characters in films, but when they are, they are disproportionately likely to be the villain—the character everyone fears, the character who is looking to do ill deeds, the character who must be thwarted or put out of his miserable, embittered existence. This is not just an occasional occurrence

This is an intvocto point

but a commonality in many of the biggest and most legendary films in cinematic history. Take, for example, the unmasked Darth Vader in *Star Wars*—sickly, breathing with labored assistance, the disabled remnants of what had been. Or Lord Voldemort from the Harry Potter series, or Gollum from *The Lord of the Rings*—both disfigured, pale-skinned, crypt-like, unwell. This is not a criticism of any of these series, as I am a huge fan of all of them, but a criticism of how we as a society have grown to associate unwellness, disfigurement, and physical abnormality with some form of evil. These are the images we see and these are the concepts we are led to understand over and over. And concepts stick; ideas become instantiated in our culture.

You don't have to live it to know it, but you perhaps have to live it to fully understand the effects of it. Because of the marginalized position to which people with disabilities are often relegated in society, it's often simply taken as given that they cannot and sometimes even should not hold positions outside of that. We have a highly medicalized view of disability—that of "the patient" possibly above all else. That's what we see and understand first—the unwellness of disability rather than the strength of it. It has happened to me on more than one occasion when someone who I do not know nor who has any understanding of my life will stop me in a store or in a park and pray over me almost like an exorcism. I understand the benevolent motivation behind this, and the fact that people want to express their concern or support for people they see as less fortunate than they are is, in essence, an act of compassion. In fact, I love this about people and wouldn't want to see that aspect of compassion fade. But there is a part of it that fortifies the social hierarchy that puts people with disabilities somewhere close to the bottom.

I have spent much of my life trying to change that narrative, to lend my voice to generations of fighters who have, through word and deed, sought to alter the prevalent view of disability. And there are many of us—people whose voices emanate from the halls of academia, from the lobbies of Congress, from the audience seats of school board meetings, from wheelchairs, from augmentative speech devices, and from nursing home beds. Disability is not necessarily analogous with medical vulnerability, though it might sometimes imply it. Disability is a sociocultural construct of which "medicine" is merely a part, incorporating an individual within a framework of policies, social structures, societal supports, and community measures that directly impact her ability to lead a full and rich life.

Injury, accidents, and disease are inevitabilities in the human existence. They are going to happen; everyone is susceptible; and they are neither sources of shame nor reasons for ostracization. In my childhood, I had no reason to believe that I would ever live a part of my life in a wheelchair, and my suspicion is that most people view their lives in a similar way. "Disability is something for someone else." But the irony is that we are all occupying some spot on the spectrum of disability (or ability), and none of these spots has an eternal seating assignment. The aging process alone changes our ability—our sight, our mobility, our hearing, our cognition—whether or not we would like it to. Just as much, fate's spin of the wheel can change our likelihood of having our abilities altered, and all that is an informal guarantee we assume upon entry into the world. While the occurrence of disability is a fact—and not a regrettable one—the effects of disability can be either mitigated or exacerbated by what we as members of society choose to do.

Disability makes life more difficult, that is undeniable, but the current construct of our society is a significant factor in the extent of just how difficult. The world we live in is fundamentally not set up for people with disabilities. When I say "set up," I mean myriad things. Our architecture is not welcoming to people with disabilities—steps into a building are the preferred option over smooth inclines, making many homes, public buildings, and stores completely inaccessible. Our education system is not built to accommodate a variety of learning styles and needs—with the common expectation for children born with disabilities being that they will either not attend a mainstream classroom or, worse yet, not attend school at all. Our jobs and means of hiring people are highly discriminatory against people with disabilities, as those who make it to an interview often proceed no further because of their ability status or fears of work-related accommodations that might have to be made. And our policies, especially those in the health and human services areas, too often create unanticipated challenges and even impossibilities for people with disabilities to live their everyday lives. The structural and societal factors that exacerbate disability have demonstrable effects on people with disabilities themselves and on how society perceives people with disabilities. In a curious irony, they can even have an impact on how people with disabilities perceive themselves. I know this to be true because I have lived it.

The transition from the life I had known as a child to the life I know now was deeply emotionally difficult because I understood my identity in terms of my physicality: the activities in which I was a part; the time I spent at my dancing school, the karate dojo, or on the soccer field; the sound of my voice. Not unlike any transformative life event—the loss of a loved one, the loss of a job—the personal transition into a wheelchair is jarring, frightening, and forces you to rethink nearly every aspect of your daily reality. But it can be done, just like people learn to live beautiful and rich lives even with the pain of the loss of a loved one in their hearts. My life over the past thirty years has been characterized by more love and opportunity and possibility and meaning than I could have envisioned, and almost as much as I would have wanted. However, for many people with disabilities, this doesn't happen nearly as often as it should.

The expectation that people with disabilities, particularly quadriplegia, might only find love in the most unlikely circumstances or are incapable of maintaining friendships or are unable to hold a job says far less about quadriplegia or the people who live with it than it says about our collective and societal understanding and appreciation of disability. A life of perceived loneliness or social marginalization or denial of opportunity should not be what we expect from a disability like quadriplegia, and no one should tolerate otherwise. There is no reason that this ought to be the presumptive outcome, and this is part of what people most fear about the potential of disability. Coincidentally, this is also what is most in our collective ability to rectify.

Living with quadriplegia is difficult, yes, but, even for me, who lives only with the assistance of a ventilator, the physicality of paralysis is only one part of a much more complex and socioculturally constructed existence. Learning to live with quadriplegia is one's own personal evolution, done on one's own personal timeline, but it is the institutionalized and systemic structures that can often make the days seem like too much to endure. This is a societal problem, not an individual problem. This is a matter of public policy, not personal policy. Until we understand that, and until society claims some degree of ownership over that, people living with quadriplegia, or any disability for that matter, will run up against barriers, injustices, and paternalistic condescension, irrespective of how much determination they might have.

"I could never live in a situation like yours; I'm not strong enough." I hear that quite frequently, and it is an injustice to everyone—people with disabilities like mine for whom the assumption is that the challenges we experience make our lives not worth it, and people without disabilities who underestimate what they can endure. It is less that people with quadriplegia don't want to live in this world than it is that the world is not set up for them to live fully in it. Whether in our education system, employment practices, urban planning, policymaking, entertainment, technology, or social inclusion, people with quadriplegia—or paralysis and even disability, generally speaking—can often be led to believe that the world would be better off without them or that accommodating their needs is a magnanimous act of charity rather than the provision of a basic civil right. People with disabilities like quadriplegia can often fall victim to the notion that their lives are somehow the inferior version of the able-bodied fortunate, and that the divide between what is and what could have been were it not for disability is something about which they should be ashamed or apologetic. People with quadriplegia are led to believe these things because nearly every aspect of our society indicates—whether implicitly or explicitly—that they are true.

The intricacies of this reality are Seurat-esque in their granularity and detail. For instance, wheelchairs are not the jailers that they are so often depicted or understood to be. Rather, they are forms of liberation and independence. I am not "confined to my wheelchair," I am empowered by it. The impediments lie in lack of attention to inclusive design and accessibility in architecture, urban planning, and economic development. Steps into a building are the "no wheelchair users allowed" signs in architectural form. This level of inaccessibility is somewhat obvious, but it goes far beyond that. The perfectly legal 14(c) exemption to the Fair Labor Standards Act which, instituted in 1938, allows employers to apply for a waiver to pay employees with disabilities up to 50 percent less than a "nondisabled" employee due to some estimated loss of productivity. Under the anachronistic conception that any inclusion of people with disabilities into the workforce is laudable charity, this is now a legislated societal admission that the disabled worker's work is and certainly must be worth less, maybe even worthless. And our children born with disability or become disabled lead their lives seeing astonishingly few people who ambulate like they do holding positions of influence or represented in the media in ways other than incapacitated or hopeless. All of these social constructions make personal advancement seem inaccessible, make personal empowerment and independence seem inaccessible, and, indeed, make the world seem inaccessible. This is a message being sent to people with disabilities like quadriplegia, but, perhaps more detrimentally, it is the message being sent to everyone in a self-fulfilling feedback loop.

We do ourselves a disservice by accepting the perception that a disability like quadriplegia is tantamount to a life of limited value and, to whatever degree or for whatever reason it might be, we do people an injustice by perpetuating the myth that people with disabilities have little or even less to offer. We also deny ourselves the opportunity to right a social wrong. Right now, there is little that can be done to address the physical limitations brought about by quadriplegia, and for some who experience it, this is not necessarily a desired or preferred outcome. However, as a society and as a population all at risk of disability, we can and must reduce systemic and institutionalized barriers so they have the least significant impact on quality of life. The needs of people with disabilities must be incorporated into every policy discussion, at every level, and not with an eye to mere accommodation but to full inclusion—in our transportation systems, in our urban design, in our education and employment practices, and in our overall pursuit for justice. Until that time comes, we will always assume that having a disability like quadriplegia is a life never wanted and a life we need to escape.

Learning to live with disability, just like learning to live at all, isn't a personal quest to the top of the mountain, it's a process of creativity buffered by a common capacity to care, both from afar and when it gets your hands the dirtiest. The mechanics of disability are merely mechanics, and these, at least, we can engineer much better than we do. It was never an inevitability that disability had to imply all of the ideas it currently does; we, as a society, collectively constructed those ideas, and they are in need of deconstruction. We can, in fact, engineer a world in which the adjective "disabled" carries no normative connotation other than one of strength and resilience, creativity and problem-solving. And those girders can become the very structure on which people with disabilities build their lives.

3

←——————→

THE FAMILY OF THE
DISABLED CHILD

Every day will be difficult, some extremely so, and some in ways that now cannot be anticipated. But the single most important piece of information I can give these families is that they can *and that people* have.

I LIVE WITH MY PARENTS. This is a status that not many forty-two-year-old adults claim, at least not publicly. There is an embarrassment that, for most, is associated with living with your parents into adulthood—an indication either that an individual has not reached the point of maturity and self-ownership to be able to live on one's own, or the indication that an individual has not been fortunate enough to find the relationships, whether intimate or otherwise, to leave the nest and start a life anew. I have internalized both of these ideas and have allowed them to negatively influence my own understanding of myself and my place in the world to a degree I often regret.

Many people with significant disabilities live with their families late into adulthood. They are the lucky ones. Many more people with significant disabilities are destined to a fate far less hopeful and even far less safe. People with significant disabilities often require care, sometimes complicated and advanced care that is necessary to keep them alive. Sometimes family members can be taught how to administer this care, but sometimes not. Sometimes the care is too medically involved for an untrained family member to provide, and instead, skilled nursing is necessary—something that, more often than not, cannot be gotten. There is a vast shortage of skilled nursing available for care provided in the home, as many health insurance companies do not provide reimbursement for this service. For those that do, the number of hours of nursing care they provide is woefully inadequate or the reimbursement rate is much lower than what a nurse might earn in a hospital. And in many instances in which nursing care or home health assistance can be gotten, the care can be so unreliable and even of such poor quality that it is as if no care is given at all. So, through no fault or desire of their own, family members of people with disabilities are often left with no choice other than to make the gut-wrenching decision to admit their family member to a medical institution.

There are many more instances in which the care of a disabled person can be taught to a family member, and there is then the possibility that this person could live at home, among her community and loved ones. But it is not so simple.

The United States has made caring for a family member nearly impossible. And this is not simply for people with disabilities, but also for parents caring for children, adults caring for elderly parents, or spouses caring for sick spouses. In an aberration from many other industrialized nations, the

U.S. has made a series of public policy decisions that privatizes this kind of care, forcing family members to provide it on an entirely uncompensated basis. If it is possible and economically feasible, a family member can be the care provider instead of being a part of the workforce. Despite the fact that caregiving is some of the most difficult, time-consuming, stressful, yet noble and rewarding work that can be done, our society has repeatedly and consistently through matters of public policy decided to make it appear valueless. Parents of disabled children, almost without exception mothers, provide billions of dollars each year in uncompensated care to their disabled children. This is not simply "billions" as in $2 billion or $3 billion, but $375 billion per year, according to the Caregiver Action Network (CAN), and this amount is almost twice as much as the $150 billion that is actually spent on home care and nursing home services combined.[5] How could we possibly arrive at such an astronomically large amount of uncompensated care that family members provide? Well, as CAN has estimated, there are more than 53 million people, or more than 15 percent of the U.S. population, who provide this kind of care for chronically ill, disabled, or elderly family members or friends, and they do this for an average of twenty hours per week. (Although there are many more who provide care for much more than twenty hours per week.) In the stunning analysis conducted by the National Alliance for Caregiving and Evercare, the researchers determined that family caregivers are the essential backbone of long-term care that is provided to people across the United States, far outpacing Medicaid long-term care spending in all states.[6]

What is interesting is that, although disability affects everyone in every demographic group, there is a strong, bidirectional correlation between disability and low-income status. Pregnant women of lower economic means sometimes do not receive adequate prenatal care or nutrition, thereby increasing the likelihood of disability for her child. Families of lower socioeconomic means sometimes live in buildings or communities where the risk of injury is greater, and as a result, the likelihood of sustaining a disabling injury is higher. On the other side of the coin, people with disabilities are often less likely to be employed and more likely to need time away from work if they are employed, thereby negatively affecting their ability to earn a decent living. These factors play a significant role in how disability is experienced across the population. But because there is a link between lower economic means or poverty and disability, the families of these individuals are the least able to voluntarily pull themselves from the workforce and provide the care that their loved ones need. And therein lies an irreconcilable problem. If the family members of people with disabilities are the best or most likely individuals to care for them but their socioeconomic means do not allow them to provide this care on an uncompensated basis, how are they to provide it?

The consequence of this is that many more people than should find themselves with no choice but to become a resident of a medicalized institution. There are, I'm sure, medical institutions in which the care is very good and residents live healthy lives. However, I'm afraid that this scenario is much more the exception than the rule. Generally speaking, despite the oversight that these facilities are subject to, the care is as frightening as one might expect it to be. A comprehensive study conducted by the Kaiser Family Foundation (KFF), a prominent health-policy research think tank, looked at the conditions of nursing home facilities in the United States. Their findings were grim but unsurprising.

According to data compiled by KFF, within the United States alone, 1.3 million individuals with disabilities live in nursing homes; 800,000 live in assisted living facilities; and 75,000 live in intermediate care facilities.[7] These numbers represent people's lives. These numbers bring with them consequences. According to KFF, nursing home facilities are severely understaffed. There is a strong correlation between the number of registered nurses employed in a nursing home and the outcome of care, but the federal government has not yet passed minimum staffing levels for these facilities. The outcome of this is that registered nurses are either taking on more patients and, thus, working more hours per resident per day, or, and likely more frequently, the care that would ordinarily be provided by registered nurses is, instead, being provided by unlicensed nursing care. Because staffing levels are tied to quality of outcome, it isn't surprising that insufficient licensed staffing, over time, has produced frightening deficiencies in care. Nursing homes are monitored on 175 requirements, and they receive requirement-specific citations if they fail to meet any of them. In 2016, the percent of nursing homes across the country that received no citations was only 6.5 percent. Fewer than one in ten and almost one in twenty. The most common deficiencies were not in inconsequential areas. They included infection control, accident environment, food sanitation, quality of care, and pharmacy consultation. According to KFF, more than one in five facilities received a deficiency that actually caused physical harm or put its residents in jeopardy. As unimaginable as these circumstances are, in themselves, they have become more consequential and more alarming, especially in recent times of crisis.[8] Very early in the COVID-19 pandemic, in April 2020, there had already been over ten thousand reported deaths due to COVID-19 in long-term care facilities, which represented 27 percent of the deaths due to the pandemic in the U.S. By November 2020, that number had jumped to one hundred thousand deaths among long-term care residents and staff. In some U.S. states, more than 50 percent of all COVID-19 deaths were among long-term care residents with disabilities.

This is the reality of the lives of many people with disabilities across the country. They face the unenviable decision of not receiving the care they need at home or receiving some subpar version of the care they need in a facility that is hazardous to their very health. This Cornelian dilemma has remained the case because we have lacked the political will to make the changes we need to rectify it.

For the time I have lived with quadriplegia, I have been spared this fate. This statement is simply a matter of fact, as well as a matter of circumstance and a matter of good fortune. Throughout the six weeks that I was in pediatric intensive care, both of my parents were at my bedside every day. They were there together through the horror of the first two weeks, when questions about my survival were far from certain—when physicians of all kinds beat a well-trafficked path in and out of my hospital room with pieces of information, each grimmer than the one before.

My parents needed to be there, and needed to be there together, as the information they were receiving from health-care professionals of all different sorts was both foreign and overwhelming, forcing them to make potentially life-altering decisions in remarkably short amounts of time. There were procedures to provide consent for, questions to ask about the future of my life, and grave uncertainties about whether, at any given moment, the devices and personal fortitude that were keeping me alive would simply run out. Neither of my parents, strong and resolved as they were, could have endured that alone.

As the weeks went by, my condition became more stable, and the fear of death or making the wrong decision became less immediate. For the remainder of the six weeks that I was in pediatric intensive care, my parents would split the hours by my bedside, with my mother spending the day with me and my father staying during the evenings.

It is difficult to shoulder the intense emotionality of a hospitalized child alone. It is almost as difficult to shoulder the emotionality of a hospitalized child when it is shared between two people, as trauma and suffering do not abide by principles of mathematics, and twice the weary shoulders does not halve the pain.

And yet, bearing the enormity of these emotions was a commitment that my family made for nine months. My mother spent the seven and a half months I was in rehabilitation in New Jersey with me. My father would come for intermittent weeks when he could get away from work, during which time my mother would return home to Long Island to be with my sister and brother, to pick out furniture and designs for the renovations that had to be done to my home to accommodate my wheelchair, and to relieve my grandmother, who was staying at my house in my mother's absence, ensuring that everyone was fed and taken care of while my mother was away with me. It was a situation that no one wanted, not any of it, but the alternative, we feared, would be much worse.

The decision my parents made for my mother to leave her job as a teacher so that I could be brought home from the hospital and cared for in my community was in no way an obvious one. The decision was obvious to my parents and family, no doubt, but it was not obvious to many others. When I arrived at rehabilitation, taken by ambulance from Stony Brook University Hospital all the way to New Jersey, the first question that was asked of my parents was whether I was being admitted for long-term care. In other words, it was assumed that I was arriving to be admitted into the nursing home facility of the hospital, likely for the remainder of my life. This was not an uncommon arrangement for children with disabilities as significant as mine. In fact, particularly in 1990 when the aesthetic surrounding disability was quite different from what it is today, this was the expected. But just because the decision that my parents made was obvious to them does not mean that it was easy for anyone.

I have been the disabled member of my family for three decades. This is not how my family understands the dynamic, but it is how I do. This interpretation is probably inaccurate and, as a result, unfair. Shortly after Reed turned thirty, he contracted a virus that attacked the auditory nerve in his left ear, leaving him with chronic bouts of vertigo and almost entirely deaf in his left ear. My parents have both sustained knee injuries, back injuries, and wrist injuries from the wear and tear of a life that is physically demanding and that few others would have the physical strength to maintain. Kysten, when she was in her twenties, was diagnosed with myasthenia gravis, which, though now in remission, could have caused neurological damage in her face. And yet, I have understood myself to be the disabled family member—the one whose life others had to, or chose to, conform theirs around. But it is much more than that.

A disabling accident or event affects an individual and it affects a family. I always knew this to be true, but as the child with the disability, it was exceptionally difficult for me to understand exactly in what ways this was true. Better said, it was exceptionally difficult for me to allow myself to understand exactly in what ways this is true.

I AM ONE OF THREE

Kysten and Reed are two-thirds of my parents' worlds. Kysten and Reed are 66 percent of the people to whom my parents have devoted their lives. These were data and figures that I always knew, and, particularly being the middle child, I always understood the logical outcome: a supposed egalitarian entitlement to one-third of my parents' time and attention. But the consequence of disability is that many of the activities of life that require essentially no time or effort for most everyone else are just the opposite for a child with a disability. And that requires time—time that does not often have to be afforded to children. For instance, after the first few years of life, children usually do not require the help of their parents to get dressed or take a shower or get ready for the day. My life over the past thirty years has required all of these things. This adds up to significant amounts of time spent with one child at the expense of the others—time my parents spent with me at the expense of my sister and brother. That is simply a fact; there is no other way to compartmentalize the time. I know how much time with my parents Kysten and Reed lost by my gain of it.

If it were only a matter of the division of time itself, that would be one thing—certainly a more easily accepted thing—but that is only part of the calculation. The thoughts of parents of children with disabilities almost always revolve around the needs of their disabled child. Throughout the most potentially memorable years of my childhood, all of the plans that were planned, outings that were outed, parties that were partied, rides that were rode were all thought out with me in mind. Decisions to do something or not to do something—take a vacation, go to the movies, go out to eat—were made with my needs in mind.

Both Kysten and Reed handled the loss differently, but both felt it in the same order of magnitude. Until my accident, Kysten and I had shared an upstairs bedroom, painted pink and adorned with pastel-colored bedding and posters of all sorts on the walls. We fought like sisters do— particularly sisters who share a confined space—and I wanted a bedroom of my own more than I wanted anything. That is, until I had no choice but to have my own bedroom—newly built on the first floor of the house.

Kysten had an especially difficult time coming to terms with the changes in our family life that were precipitated by my accident. Kysten is not, and was not, a noted enthusiast of change, and the changes that my family and I were undergoing were easily many more than many thirteen-year-olds might ever embrace, but this was particularly challenging for Kysten. While she did not witness my accident taking place, she did come to the scene of the accident and saw for herself my mangled body on the

Nicolls Road concrete. While she was not the daughter who was physically injured, she was no less mentally and emotionally traumatized by circumstances that were beyond her control and beyond the realm of her understanding. Kysten was terrified of life's fragility, the extent of which she was forced to see especially acutely, and she was angry over the seemingly arbitrary nature by which circumstances changed and injustice was made manifest. "Why did this happen to our family?" "Why do we have to deal with this?"

These are not surprising questions and frustrations from a thirteen-year-old trying to make sense of trauma. These are especially not surprising questions and frustrations from a thirteen-year-old trying to make sense of trauma that did not—at least not visibly—directly affect her. There is a conflict of multiple manifestations of guilt—guilt about being the uninjured child; guilt about resenting attention redistributed to the disabled sibling; guilt about wanting things different than they were—the same as they had been.

Like many other siblings of children with disabilities, Kysten was angry. She was angry about how many parts of our lives had been uprooted and changed irrevocably. Not only had Kysten and I shared a bedroom, we had shared many fundamental aspects of our lives. The two of us were dancers together; Kysten started when she was three years old and I started when I was just two years old. The year of my accident was to be my tenth year as a dancer, though I was only eleven years old, and Kysten's eleventh year, though she was only thirteen—a momentous year for both of us in the lives that revolved around our dancing. After my accident, though, Kysten could not and did not want to return to dancing school. It was something that we shared, something that one could not do without the other. For the 1990–91 school year, the year in which I was in the hospital, Kysten was in ninth grade, the oldest class of the seventh, eighth, and ninth grade junior high school. She was bombarded by questions about how I was doing in the hospital, what kind of progress I was making, and when I was going to come home. She knew as little as any of us when it came to any of those questions. The fact of the matter was that she was grieving her losses and was in as much pain as anyone, and those questions could have been asked of her just as easily as they were asked about me. This was an understanding that I didn't have at the time.

While I was in the rehabilitation hospital in New Jersey, Kysten came to visit me a few times early on but then stopped. I didn't know why and could not, for the life of me, understand it. There were some weekends when I thought she simply did not want to be bothered, other weekends when I thought she was angry with me for my foolishness and for putting our family through all it had to go through. I know now how deeply I misunderstood the directionality of this anger. This anger has become familiar to me, as I see it on the faces and in the words of many other siblings of children with disabilities to whom I've spoken over the years. It is an anger directed at the cavernous gap between the life we want and the life we have. It is a frustration over an inability to change things in the way you would want to see them changed. It is a violation of every cause-and-effect lesson that may have been learned up until that time—that by doing *x*, you can get *y* result—because no matter how many times you try to do *x*, *y* remains tauntingly beyond your grasp. And it is a fear that, at any given moment, things can, once again, go wildly awry and change all that you had become accustomed to. I understand this now. I wish I had understood this then.

It takes no higher learning in psychology or human behavior to know that anger is often a mask for the more complex and difficult-to-isolate emotion of sadness. My brother, Reed, was the youngest of all of us, but he was also the wisest and, because of that, the most able to understand

Do you think that, from all the lessons and understandings you've come through—there could have been a way to speed run/short-circut this? How can disabled kids [?] further be helped to see these things the way you have w/o having to go through all that the hard way?

the heaviness of what he was experiencing. He was also the one most able to manage those emotions and reinterpret them in a way that changed both of our lives for the better.

Reed was only ten years old in 1990, having just turned ten at the beginning of the summer. While I shared a bedroom with Kysten, throughout our childhood, Reed and I were veritably and willingly tethered to each other. There is no better friend I could have asked for. When I danced, Reed was my favorite audience. When he played the piano, he was my favorite musician. We spent nearly every evening on the den floor together, executing an adventure or envisioning a new one. He was my best friend, and I had no doubt that I was his.

When your best friend is injured as badly as my brother's best friend was, the grief is not only all-consuming, but multiplicatively all-consuming, upending different facets of your life in the same gut-wrenching way. There is the grief that is immediately felt by the injury, as if the distance between my heart and his were any sort of formidable barrier. And then there is the grief that all that had been known and was real and fundamental to who you are is simply gone, never to return. There is the pain of loss in every way that the heart can feel loss. This is true for all best friends grieving losses, but evermore so when that best friend also comes in the form of your sister and even more than that when this loss means that your most reliable and steadfast sources of comfort no longer have the time or energy to provide all of the comfort you need.

This is the existence Reed was thrown into without warning or explanation. At just ten years old, Reed had to learn to absorb the loss of his childhood and the loss of his best friend, at least in the form that he knew her. But he did this with a grace and rapidity that far exceeded his years. In almost no discernible amount of time at all, Reed was looking for ways that the difference my injury had created did not have to be understood as a disparity. Reed was a young child, only beginning to learn the math skills that he would master and carry into his adulthood and career, but he was wise enough to know that "not equal" did not mean "less than." So, starting immediately in his first trip to visit me in rehabilitation, we adapted. We modified that which was modifiable. We rethought that which we could rethink. We held on to the foundation and built from there.

Reed and I spent the years of our lives in which many siblings grow apart growing together. The hours that may very well have transformed from playing on the den floor into hours fighting for bathroom rights or telephone time instead transformed into hours working together on logic problems or crossword puzzles or challenging each other to games of Scrabble. In the evenings after school, I would watch at the end of the driveway while Reed would play basketball or work on his volleyball serves. This shifting of roles and adaptation of relationship was, perhaps, not the way either of us anticipated our lives evolving, but the fact of the matter was that it would have evolved in some way whether or not my accident had ever taken place, and quite possibly in a direction that could have divided us far more than this one united us.

But none of this, however, could fully alleviate the sadness of a childhood lost or at least a childhood eroded too soon. And with this loss of childhood came a loss of opportunity and innocence. It has only been in recent years that Reed told me that during times when my parents were in my bedroom with me providing care—changing my tracheostomy tube, suctioning my lungs, getting me into or out of bed—he would lie in his own bedroom, studying the globe, quizzing himself on presidential legacies or historical arcana, waiting for familial life that included him to resume. Reed has told me on many occasions that he was not ever upset by this and that it never impacted his development. I wish I believed that were true.

Reed was soldier-like after my accident. He cared for me and was compassionate in ways I still have yet to fully comprehend. But implicit in that care and compassion for me was a commensurate reduction in time and attention for him. I needed my parents in ways that I never had before, but so, too, did Kysten and Reed. They were strong for me when I felt that I was weak, but I, whether by nature or by circumstance, was not fully able to see the need to do the reverse. While I view my life in hindsight with pride, I also cannot escape—nor would I want to—the remorse of missing those emotional voids when I could have helped to fill them. I understand that now. I wish I had understood this then.

I lost an enormous amount in my accident: my ability to walk, my ability to dance, my ability to breathe, my ability to take part in many of the rites of passage that come to define one's life. Reassessing and then, as a result, relearning to live my life was inordinately hard—perhaps unimaginably hard—and is a process that might never fully reach its completion. For me, though maybe not for all, breathing through a ventilator is something that will never feel natural. It is something I might never get used to. But for much longer than I ever should have, I drew a false correlation between what these losses meant for me and what they should mean for everyone else in my family.

For years after my accident, I did myself and my family an enormous injustice that has only—and most unfortunately—become visible in retrospect. For years after my accident, especially throughout the remaining years of my childhood, I thought of myself as the one who others needed to feel sorry for because that's what I thought you were supposed to do for the rare person you might see in a wheelchair—feel sorry for her. For years after my accident, I thought of myself as the one who, by fate or misfortune, was simply left holding the undesired end of the stick. While I was happy to be the one to have borne the brunt of the suffering, I thought that since neither my sister nor brother were paralyzed, they were the lucky ones, or at least the luckier ones. The amount of care and time that my life demanded from my parents seemed to me to be just a consequence of the losses I had sustained. The seemingly incessant barrage of strangers coming into and going out of my house on a regular basis—nurses, therapists, medical-supply deliverymen, wheelchair repairmen—just seemed to be a part of life that everyone would have to get used to. The wheelchair lockdowns in the van, the hours-per-day of medical care, the vacations that were not taken, the backyard that was decked over to accommodate my wheelchair, the holidays that had to be rearranged, the house that had to be reconstructed—all of these things, all of these immeasurably impactful aspects of my family's lives, I thought, were simply the outcome of my life's changed circumstances and things that others would just have to acclimate to because they were the luckier ones.

I am often asked if there are parts of my life I would want to do over or change—with the expected answer being that I would change my decision to walk home from school on September 4, 1990. But if I had to choose, I would change how I understood myself, especially in relation to my family in those years immediately after my accident, and how unfairly I evaluated the magnitude of my loss over anyone else's and then fundamentally misunderstood everyone else's needs as a result.

In the decades that I have lived with quadriplegia, I have had this conversation with my parents many times. When I was younger, I was not strong enough or sure enough of myself to ask what boundaries I needed to put on my needs, which were considerable and time-consuming, versus the limitations I could reasonably expect my family to put on their needs by virtue of my own. This understanding has come with time but not with ease.

I live with my parents, and we are currently a party of three, whose table seats at least two more. This life we lead, even all these years after my accident, constantly requires reevaluation, course correction, creativity, flexibility, and humor. But it also produces anxiety, stress, frustration, and moments of such theretofore unreleased exasperation that all you can do is either scream or burst into tears. But we have done this with a grace and resolve that no one ever expects to have to demonstrate. My parents are the strongest people I could ever hope to know and the most steadfast. We eat dinner at an embarrassingly early 4:00 p.m. every day almost without fail, because my parents start their day at the frighteningly early 4:00 a.m., every day without fail. Their lives are hard but purposeful. Their spirits are youthful, but they are getting older, and I wake up every single morning terrified that something may have happened to one of them during the night. My accident upended both of my parents' lives and altered their expectations of what our familial future might look like, but they have embraced it without ever indicating that the circumstances we have collectively faced were either too much to bear or too little like they had hoped. Undoubtedly, my mother's life is the life that has been most indirectly influenced by the direct hit I took. But now, some thirty years later, our lives are so intertwined and seamlessly interwoven that they are almost one and the same. My oldest nephew, Carter, calls my mother and me "Nee-Nee-Brookie-Nee-Nee" or, just to cover all bases, "Brookie-Nee-Nee-Brookie," as if we were one entity in two bodies. He isn't wrong. That kind of giving of yourself to the life of someone else is the kind of sacrifice that only parents make. Both of my parents have told me that what they have done for me is "not a sacrifice," but I know better than that. I know what sacrifice is and I know what they have done to make my life what it is, and I see no functional difference between the two.

MOMS AND DADS OF DISABLED KIDS

When you are the parent of a disabled child and you accept the terms of that arrangement, the unanticipated consequence of that relationship is the need to fight. Nearly everything that is desired for your child—and is unquestionably provided to other children—is the result of a fight: their education, their basic health-care needs, their ability to participate in their communities, and even their basic well-being. All these necessities that seem so obvious to any parent as fundamental rights and expectations for their children are, far more often than not, only the result of hard-fought battles.

The first battle that my parents fought occurred before I left the rehabilitation hospital, and they haven't stopped since. It was just one day before I was scheduled to be released after seven and a half months of seeing my family only on the weekends, seeing my friends rarely if ever, and longing to be home among the people I loved. During that time, I had learned to speak while also breathing through a ventilator. I had learned to drive a wheelchair. I had surgery to stabilize my spine. I had learned to be an adult in a child's body. And I was ready—*dying*—to go home.

I was scheduled to leave the hospital on May 15, a day that seemed almost too good to be true. The night before, my father had called my mother at the hospital to tell her that there had been a problem. The nurses who were scheduled to be at my house when I came home the next day could not be coordinated, and because of that, I would have to stay in rehabilitation, unclear for exactly how long. It was devastating news. I had my bags packed, I had said my goodbyes, I had planned what I would do and say first and to whom when I arrived home. Then, my greatest fears became a reality—that the day I had been yearning for, the moment I had been waiting for was not really going to happen, that it was all just a fantasy.

That was one of the most salient moments in my life. I had already learned to fight for my survival, but those were internal battles. It was at that moment that my family and I knew that our fights for survival were going to be external also. While my mother consoled me, despite being heartbroken herself, my father called the nursing agency, the insurance company, the case coordinator, family, friends, and doctors, in a fury. This was never to happen again. This incompetence and even negligence was never to happen again. All these entities had to assure my father that I would be home within a week and that no mistakes would be made again.

The experience we gained from that first battle was necessary to build the resilience for battles to come.

Over the years, my parents battled my school district when they told my family, without even a moment's hesitation, that my inclusion in a mainstream classroom would be inappropriate and disruptive to my fellow classmates. "A homeschool setting is much better for your daughter," they explained, as if they had a better sense of what was best for me. My parents fought that. My parents battled health insurance companies that refused to pay for basic and necessary medical supplies for my survival or wheelchairs so I could get around. "These items are luxuries," they explained, as if the ability to breathe, avoid infection, or leave my bedroom were unreasonable wants akin to the yachts and private jets that the CEOs of these companies might have. My parents fought that. My parents battled with medical-supply companies that, when they did not get the reimbursement rate they wanted, would fail to deliver supplies or send bills to us for the amount they did not receive. "We have to be able to run our business," they would explain, as if the health-care-by-profit bottom line ought to carry more weight than the human bottom line. My parents fought that. My parents battled stores and restaurants and theaters and even cities that were not accessible to me. "These places aren't designed for your daughter," they would explain, as if civil rights were the outcome of architectural whim or design preference rather than something basic and fundamental and the product of being a citizen. My parents fought that too.

These battles are exhausting and tiresome at the same time—exhausting because they demand so much more energy than necessary when additional energy is already at a premium, and tiresome because they are so repetitive, so monotonous, and so mind-numbingly banal that it is almost as if you are in a battle of wills with an automaton. But my parents have taken on these battles and continue to do so, not simply for me but also in the event that a decision that is made for me by virtue of their efforts might set the precedent for others. So while my biggest regret in retrospect is how I misunderstood my needs in relation to those of my family, my biggest source of pride is how my family—each one of us—confronted immeasurable odds, stared them down, and said *step aside*.

As proud and as willing as my parents are to take on these battles, I know that they have taken their toll. The parent of a disabled child is hypervigilant, always on alert for what might go wrong next, always wary of where a potential adversary might lie. And this constant surveillance—this continual patrolling of environments or taking up of arms against wrongdoers—is extremely difficult to maintain. But for many parents of disabled children, theirs are the hands that will offer protection, theirs are the eyes that will keep watch.

This sense of protectionism never really goes away. You never age out of it. For some disabled people, their survival is the result of it. And yet, there have been some, even those within the disability studies circles, who have criticized the role that parents play in the lives of kids with disabilities—that they are overbearing, overprotective, too outspoken, too frazzled. But that criticism comes from a blatant misunderstanding of the day-to-day lives that families with disabilities lead. Over the years, my family and I have been contacted by many families with recently injured or newly diagnosed children. Many of these children have been diagnosed with quadriplegia, whether from a spinal cord injury, a bout with disease, or a congenital condition, and these families are terrified. They have been thrown into a set of circumstances they were not expecting and which seem completely foreign. There is no guidebook or instruction manual for how to make a life with a disabled child. Parents can be taught to operate a wheelchair, to insert a catheter, to change a bandage. But there are no lessons on how to live and how to thrive.

I have sat around the kitchen table or in the coziness of a living room with many parents of disabled children. The look on their faces is nearly always the same: It is a unique weariness from concern and uncertainty coupled with a unique readiness to always be on guard. This was the same wariness and readiness that lined my parents' faces years ago, a look that has only modestly lessened with time. But these parents come to my home or I go to theirs, and we talk. . . .

We talk about fear. Many parents of children with disabilities are plagued with fear. And this is to be expected, without question. They are fearful of doing something wrong, of creating additional injury through a mistake or misstep. The care for a disabled child is as innate as the care for any child, but the execution of that care is much more difficult and much less intuitive. But these fears dissipate with experience. It does not take long before the care that is provided to a disabled child is just as back-of-the-hand as the care provided to any other child. That is a lesson that comes from love and with dedication. But these immediate fears are often masks for deeper and less tangible fears that every parent, but particularly the parents of disabled children, have. These parents are fearful of what their children's futures will be and how they will get there. There is a chronological dimension to these fears: How do we continue to live in difficulty every day, for all of our days? There is an opportunity dimension to these fears: How will my child become all of the things that she wants to be and I want her to be? There is a protection dimension to these fears: How will I keep my child from the slings and arrows that life surely has in its arsenal, and how can I continue to keep them away when I am no longer here to do that myself? There is an injustice dimension to these fears: Why should I have to be afraid of all of these things to begin with, when no one else I know has to? And there is an existential dimension to these fears, a dimension only fully understood by those in the throes of the experience and the one most haunting: How do we live our lives like they are our lives again?

Every parent of a disabled child with whom I have been in contact fears these very same things. They are the essential questions about what it will take to get through all the remaining days when none of these days looks anything like the days before. There is a pain deeply embedded in these fears—both a pain for the child who will have to live her life potentially vastly different than everyone else, but also a pain for the parent who will have to do likewise. There is no remedy for that pain because it is a part of the human heart that is always in existence but most often never has to be tapped into. But all of the dimensions of these fears have their antidote in hope.

I would never delude families that I speak to that the life they have ahead will be easy. In fact, I tell them quite the opposite, that life will be more exhausting, strenuous, complicated, and frustrating for you than it will be for most others you know. Every day will be difficult, some extremely so, and some in ways that now cannot be anticipated. But the single most important piece of information I can give these families is that they *can* and that people *have*. Life has moments of tremendous hardship, so much so that it feels like tears have permanent residence on the length of your cheeks. Pretending that they are not there or that they are not the product of true frustration would be to deny a fundamental aspect of humanity and human experience. But after that is over—after the tears have been shed and sleepless nights have lost their grip—you get to work. You start by realizing that "disability" will always be a characteristic of your family's life, but it is not your entire life and it does not diminish your life. There is a life to be lived and things to be done that are in no way made inferior by being the parent of a disabled child.

Disability has an omnipresence, but it does not have to be an all-consuming one, nor is it necessarily a regrettable one. It is easy to feel as if the necessary limitations that disability cause are relevant to every part of our lives—our ability to socialize, our ability to laugh, our ability to love, our ability to seize the world and make a difference in it. To believe those things is to give those limitations much more power and credit than they ever ought to have. This is not knowledge that immediately or even completely bestows itself upon the minds of families of disabled children, or their disabled children themselves. This is knowledge that comes from doing and from going.

Hope is the antidote to fear, and hope comes from the doing and the going. There is a sense of empowerment that grows out of the visualization of a battle that must be fought, fighting it, and, at times, winning it. There is a feeling of pride and empowerment that comes from successfully taking on an obstacle, a belief that, since it has been done once, it can be done again. And that knowledge is self-sustaining. The taking on of challenges, the setting of goals, and the achievement of those goals or reduction of those challenges can become a way of life. It can become a way of identifying and understanding yourself: a fighter; a goal-setter; a doer of things unexpected. And through this iterative process of setting and achieving goals, understanding the challenges before you and addressing them head-on, we all give ourselves the opportunity to be stronger than we ever thought we could be. Once that becomes part of who you are, the battle is worth fighting.

Brooke on a Foundation for a Better Life billboard campaign,
which began in September 2001.

4

←——————→

INVISIBILITY AND INFANTILIZATION

When you live with quadriplegia, you learn very quickly that many of the things you thought you could never live without, you, in fact, can.

I AM HARD TO MISS. My wheelchair is over five feet long, end to end, with a ventilator attached to the back, so my presence in any particular room doesn't often go unnoticed. There have been times when I've tried to hide from friends and family, lurking around corners or behind walls, but my attempts at inconspicuousness essentially never fool anyone. I don't mind that. In fact, the obviousness of my presence, whether in a room or in a group or out in the community, is something I relish in. I have come to enjoy putting myself front and center when the occasion warrants it—so much so that, if I am attending a conference or event at which I don't have to give a speech or presentation, I start to get jittery.

This fondness for attention and visibility is a character trait I have developed only in the second half of my life. It was by no means congenital; to the contrary, my life as a child was characterized by a shyness or introversion that held me back from many of the parts of myself I would have wanted to embrace. Or maybe I was not shy or introverted. Maybe, and more likely, I was actually quite extroverted but without the sense of self-assuredness I needed to put my extroversion into action. That self-assuredness grew over time, and I couldn't possibly overstate the importance of this aspect of my personality in the life I have led with quadriplegia.

It was my second year of graduate school at the Harvard Kennedy School of Government, where I was studying for a master in public policy, focusing on leadership and negotiation. I was there to learn more about the world and the global dynamics that shape the lives of the people in it. The life I would ultimately end up putting most acutely under the microscope, though, was my own.

I was taking a course entitled "Exercising Leadership: Mobilizing Group Resources," which would come to be the single most transformative class I would take throughout my entire education. The class was composed of some of the most talented, compassionate, and ambitious people who would enter my life. The Harvard Kennedy School houses a vast student body that is headed for leadership positions of all kinds— some interested in humanitarian work, some in nonprofit work, some in diplomacy, some in the military, some in public administration, and some in politics. The students in this particular class were of all ages and from all backgrounds, some right out of college pursuing their master in public policy or master in public administration and some "mid-career" students, who had returned to the classroom after gaining years of experience in the workforce.

The leadership course was run like a social experiment. Twice a week, we would enter the stadium-style lecture hall, name cards placed immediately in front of us, often with visible trepidation. There are many courses in the Harvard University course catalog that have been, and for good reason, described as "intense," and this qualifier is understood to apply to the course's academic rigor or workload. As a Harvard undergraduate majoring in cognitive neuroscience, I enrolled in many of them. But this leadership course was intense in a way I had never experienced intensity. The course was designed to operate like a microcosm of the dynamics that occur in society across lines of race, ethnicity, gender, sexuality, and religion. The social organization of our cultures and our communities are fractal-like, replicating themselves over and over as if they were mirror images of each other, differing only in the contextual details. In the classroom, the same dynamics of societal organization were allowed to—indeed, encouraged to—play themselves out. Alliances would be formed, hierarchies would be established, some voices would be heard at the expense of others, some conversations would be had because others were thought to be less relevant. People would fill the roles within the class that they also filled in the society at large. And this replica of society would allow students to see themselves as built-to-scale models of their personas in real life, only within the safety of the confines of the classroom, and understand their place within an overall argument, develop the skills to successfully make alliances to take on important work, and test interventions that they may not have otherwise had confidence to execute.

All of us have grandiose visions of how we might behave in times of significant emotional pressure or when our sensibilities have been challenged. "Well, I know I would have said . . ." or "Oh, I would have been like . . ." And our imagined selves embodying our envisioned responses so often are our strongest selves embodying our wittiest, cleverest, most finely tuned, and best-researched responses. Without practice, prepara-tion, self-reflection, and self-questioning, so rarely do our actual selves resemble our envisioned ones. This leadership course provided the prac-tice, preparation, self-reflection, and self-questioning needed to bring actuality and imagination into closer alignment: an actual experience, fraught with all of the stressors, anxieties, and doubts that life presents, only within the classroom walls.

As is often the case in groups, especially groups of highly motivated people, the women in the class began to feel like their voices were being drowned out by those of their male counterparts, and that their presence in and contributions to the classroom were being ignored or undervalued. Many women in the class had seen these dynamics before and had grown tired of it. The domination of the discussion by alpha males in the class, in conjunction with conversation that was framed in masculine terms and by masculine ideas, left many women in the class feeling sidelined. These dynamics, in a classroom setting, allow students to use their growing lead-ership skills to take action and effectuate change in how society operated.

The action that my female classmates took was to mobilize the women in the class to stage an intervention. Through an email chain, they chose a day and time during leadership class when the women would stand up, leave their seats, and walk to the front of the classroom, where they would stand in silent protest. The symbolism would be clear and would be strong: that the women were essential parts of the group yet they were being silenced by the very dynamics of the group. Women were essential to the group's functioning, yet their ideas, their thoughts, their perspectives, and their caveats were not being taken into account. The orchestration of this intervention was skillful, done unbeknownst to many of the men in the course. It was also done unbeknownst to me.

I was seated in the back of the classroom where, given the room's stadium-style configuration, a spot was cleared for wheelchair users. In the middle of what I thought was a fairly commonplace conversation among classmates, I watched as, one by one, the women stood up and made their way to the front of the classroom. Like the men in the room, it took me a few minutes to orient myself and realize what was taking place. The statement they were making was clear. The statement they were making was amplified by their unity—women standing shoulder to shoulder, together.

And yet, there I found myself in the back of the classroom, unaware of what was going on. Unaware of any of the coordination that had preceded it. I watched as woman after woman stood up in unity and in rebellion, making their unstated statement and calling to attention the injustice they were experiencing. I watched as my classmates were bringing to life something powerful and important, but something that did not include me. As clear as the statement was that was being made to the class, there was as clear a statement being made to me: that I was not seen as one of them.

I would never suggest or even imply that this was done intentionally. My classmates at the Harvard Kennedy School are some of the most progressive, inclusive, and justice-oriented people I have ever been surrounded by, and the relationships I built there are among the most precious in my life. But the way that disability has been understood in society is so deeply interwoven into our perceptions and behaviors that sometimes it is nearly impossible to extricate ourselves from it, no matter how inclusive we think our thinking might be. Sometimes it is easier to see the manifestation of injustice at the systemic level than it is to see injustice at the personal level. I was and am a woman, everyone knew that. When talking about me, people use the feminine pronouns: she, her, hers. None of that was in question. But I was being seen as a disabled person above all else, and that status of "disabled" was viewed not in addition to but, rather, in lieu of all other identities that were of equal significance to me.

Many of us live with intersecting identities, but disability is a camouflaging one. It can conceal all other aspects of one's identity so that the disability facet of what is necessarily a far more complex and multilayered understanding of oneself supersedes all others. Disability simultaneously makes you unusually obvious and, at the same time, incredibly invisible. Disability magnifies visibility in the way people typically understand "visibility"—the things that are physically seen and obvious to those viewing from the outside. My wheelchair, ventilator, and physical structure are all unmissable. There are almost no ways that I am able to hide in a room. However, at the same time, disability obscures so many of the other parts of myself that I often wish were just as obvious to others.

The practical implications of this dichotomy is that I, like many other people who live with disability, am often praised for my "courage," "strength," "bravery," and "determination" that many people think are the prerequisites for living life with a disability. I have spent thirty years of my life on the receiving end of this praise—being told that I am strong and courageous and inspiring. There are many people within the disability community who find this kind of praise offensive or ableist because it simplifies their lives to be no more than sources of comparison and perspective for how difficult or easy nondisabled people's lives are. I understand that interpretation, but I do not agree with it, nor have I ever. As far as I have understood it, there is no single more important accomplishment we can lay claim to in our lives than to provide someone else with the sense of empowerment to live their lives in a more productive or compassionate way. But on the other hand, this kind of praise is somewhat superficial. It requires no more than what one sees on the surface and can falsely convince people that they have come to understand what the lives of disabled people are actually like.

I take pride in my strength and courage and bravery and determination, all of which I know are part of my character and have seen me through some of the darkest points of my life. When people commend me on these characteristics, I'm not offended, and I feel quite privileged to be recognized for them. I am under no illusion that, were it not for my disability, these aspects of who I am and how I live my life would ever have become salient or signature character traits. There are aspects of our character that we don't realize exist until we need them. But to recognize any of these qualities and only these qualities is also to fail to dig any deeper as to who I am and what I care about.

I have years of experience with people knowing of me but not necessarily knowing me. I look back on my life and I know that I have missed out because of that, just as others have missed out by not getting to know more about me. The manifestations of this invisibility have evolved over the thirty years that I have lived with quadriplegia, taking various forms depending on those I am surrounded by and what is important at the time. When I was a child, first learning to adjust myself to life with a disability, I had precious few friends—one or two with whom I was very close, maybe a few more who I knew a bit more superficially. Some of my closest friends were my family and the adults—nurses, school aides, school nurses, physical therapists—who came into my life, often because that was their job. I would traverse the halls of my junior high school and my high school, saying hello to many and many more saying hello also, and that sometimes seemed good enough. But with the exception of a select few, the inseparable, life-defining friendships that characterize adolescents were not characteristic of my adolescence. And in many ways, I don't know if many people thought there was anything wrong with or unexpected about that. For certain, my family would have wanted nothing more than for my life and home to be filled with friends—friends of my age—but that fundamental need, that aspect of myself, that part of who I am went invisible to many of those around me.

And for years of my life, that was simply how it was. There were aspects of adolescence and early adulthood that I simply knew nothing of because, though they would have pertained to me as an adolescent or young adult, they lost their pertinence when the "disabled" modifier was introduced. There were friendships I didn't ever get to make. There were parties I didn't ever get invited to. There were camping trips, ski trips, and long days spent at the beach that live only in my imagined memories, not my actual ones. There are times when I regret that and wish opportunities that had been provided to others were also provided to me. But these are filaments of the past, not the foundations of my present or future.

Now, years later, I take my nephews to a local beach on the North Shore of Long Island. It is a community beach, with playgrounds for the children who have had their fill of the Long Island Sound water, board-walks and paths for cyclists and couples carrying out romantic visions of oceanside strolls, tables and chairs for picnickers. We often go at dusk, so my nephews can play while my sister, brother-in-law, brother, sister-in-law, parents, and I watch the sunset. On every visit, the beach, its paths, and its playgrounds are laced with groups of teenagers, frolicking in the sand, exaggerating their laughter, chasing each other behind the dunes. There have been moments when I have cried, wishing I had that as part of my adolescent memories, wishing that I had been invited to do those very same things in whatever way I could. But then I look at my nephews, who have lived all of their lives with me in it, my wheelchair as familiar to them as are my face and voice—"Aunt Brookie," who would do any-thing for them without a second's hesitation and whose disability is utterly meaningless to how much she loves them—and my tears of remorse are supplanted by tears of pride and faith.

Nevertheless, as an adult, the manifestation of invisibility due to disability has changed. I was having a conversation with a friend of mine, a woman who serves with me on the board of directors of the New York Civil Liberties Union, and she mentioned to me how, as people get older, they become more and more invisible—their needs are much more likely to go unrecognized, their perspectives on matters are much more likely to go unheard, opportunities that had once been afforded to them stop presenting themselves, their insights become far less valued. All of these observations are true, I acknowledged, but they are also often a way of life when you live with a disability.

My friend and I were talking about committees and groups and the role that they play in how much of the work in an organization ultimately gets done. But I explained that people with disabilities are so rarely ever seen as valuable contributors to these groups. It is sometimes the case that others believe that asking someone with a disability to do more than the bare minimum is overburdensome or beyond their capabilities. For others, it simply never occurs to them that people with disabilities would want to participate and, as a result, never even are asked. This dynamic has presented itself time and time again throughout my life—in boards I have served on, in networks I have been a part of, at jobs I have held. Disability becomes an implicit barrier between basic desires that are common across all humanity and the opportunities that anyone would want to be afforded, and an individual's ability to actually realize these desires or seize these opportunities. Not only is this interpretation of disability unnecessary, but no one is better off as a result of it.

When I was younger, I never had the feeling of self-empowerment to claim my territory or disclose these feelings or frustrations I had in my heart. They would well up and erupt in inappropriate or maladaptive ways. But now, as an adult, I am better able to synthesize my feelings and express them in a way that properly reflects their depth.

A disability like quadriplegia assumes, for some, a status of infantilization: that because some of my daily needs resemble the needs of a baby, that is how I should expect to be treated or seen. The manifestations of infantilization are far more insidious than most might be aware.

Like many people with disabilities, I am often talked down to. People approach me and ask my mother questions about me, speaking in the third person as if I were not there. "Does she need help?" "Is she finished?" This is not uncommon, and I have grown used to it. People approach me and talk unusually loudly, speaking in the simplest of phrases and using explanatory hand gestures as if I'm unable to understand their meaning without visual representation. People approach me and pat or rub my head like they would that of a child. This is not necessarily offensive to me, though I know it is to many people with similar disabilities. I understand the motivation behind it, the trepidation that people have when it comes to disability, the fear that they might embarrass themselves by doing or saying something that will not or cannot be met with a response. The thinking goes something like, "I see this person in a wheelchair, and I don't know if this person has the ability to talk, communicate, or think, and so as to avoid any embarrassing situation for me, I will cater to the lowest level of ability I can envision, and if it is something else above and beyond that, no harm done." I understand this, and I know it to be the product of the fundamental human fear of embarrassment rather than something more calculated or malevolent. I have grown accustomed to this and counteract it not by questioning the behavior but by providing strong evidence to the contrary. If that were where the story ended, it would be quite manageable and it would be the result of misunderstanding rather than malice. But there is *another* version of the infantilization of disability that is different, that does not stem from misunderstanding of what an individual with a disability is capable of doing. There is another version of this appraisal that is predicated on our basest human emotions and manifests itself in acts of marginalization and bigotry. It is this different, uglier side that, for much of my life, I had been shielded from. Protected from, as best and as long as my parents and family could protect me.

My job today as an associate professor of medical and science ethics places me in the fields of academia. Academia is where I have chosen to build my professional life, with the desire to make a contribution to collective knowledge and thought based on what I have learned and what I have experienced. I study, I research, I write, I teach, all with the aim of better understanding how the world works and influencing minds interested in the same things. The pinnacle of academia, or at least one of the pinnacles, is being risen to the position of tenure. Better said, one of the pinnacles of academia is having conducted the work and having contributed enough to collective knowledge to be granted tenure. Tenure is a status that is not frequently given, and is given only after a shockingly arduous trial-by-fire process. It requires years of research and writing, demonstration to peers—both known and unknown—of your contributions to the field in which you study, documentation of every course you have taught, paper you have written, conference you have participated in, course evaluation you have received, and award you have earned. Then the file that includes all of this information is reviewed and evaluated by a confidential committee of experts who conduct an up-or-down vote on whether or not they believe the candidate is deserving of the status. This vote is not a mere formality, and the consequences of the vote are significant. Candidates pursuing tenure who do not meet the standards set by the evaluation committee often are asked to leave the institution at which they work. This happens frequently.

The prospect of pursuing tenure is both thrilling and terrifying. Tenure brings with it the status of "senior faculty" and, likely more importantly for most, a permanent job in a discipline in which job security is tenuous and egos are large. In November 2017, I approached my colleague and supervisor, Carlos Vidal, explaining that I believed I was ready to go up for tenure and would like to begin the process—a process that can take well over a year to complete.

Throughout that entire winter, with the help of my parents, I compiled every article I had ever written, my PhD dissertation, every student evaluation and letter I received from former students, documentation from every conference I attended, every syllabus I created, every piece of my heart and soul that I had dedicated to my job. But there was no way to separate my academic career from the deep personal ties I had to Stony Brook University and the centrality of education and academia to my life and achievements. So, in addition to all my academic work, I included every article that had ever been written about me, photos of every award I had received, documentation of my honorary doctorates from Misericordia University and Rutgers University, letters from former U.S. presidents, videos from my state senate campaign, all of the things that made me who I was as a human being, above and beyond who I was as an academic. After months of compiling all these materials, the resulting file consumed five three-inch orange binders, whose color was chosen specifically to reflect my spirit, that collectively contained everything that was important in relation to my contributions to the world. I am under no illusions that quantity is a fair representation of quality, but I also know that what was contained in those binders was extraordinary. Something unlike any other tenure file.

I was granted tenure. I was granted tenure by a committee that voted unanimously in favor of it. I was granted tenure after receiving letters from colleagues in institutions across the country, some of the most over-whelmingly complementary words that have been spoken or written about me, from people I respect deeply. I received the letter finalizing my tenure from the chancellor of the State University of New York in October 2018, just weeks before my fortieth birthday. But the time between when I started the process and when it concluded was fraught with venom, hostility, and bigotry, the likes of which I had never seen or encountered in my life—the likes of which were so noxious and damaging to me that it, in fact, became questionable whether or not I would actually live to see my fortieth birthday.

Academia is a competitive place. It is competitive to the point of toxicity because nearly everyone in it considers herself to be an expert. But on top of that, in academia the consequences of abhorrent behavior are fairly small. Organizations like the military or a medical unit simply could not tolerate vindictive or self-serving behavior because it is to the detriment of all the work that takes place. In academia, self-interest is high and the consequences of it are almost nonexistent. An environment like this has people always looking over their shoulders and surprisingly ready to operate at someone else's expense.

The announcement of the fact that I was pursuing tenure unleashed a torrent of some of the most blatant bigotry I had ever encountered personally. I anticipated some viciousness and calculated competitiveness from my colleagues; this was academia, and rivalry can often be the foundation of the culture. It is part of the game, and I understand it and I'm not intimidated by it. But this was something entirely different in both genus and species. This was something rooted in a baseness that spoke much less of rivalry than it spoke of implicit evaluations of my abilities versus those of others. Some colleagues would not talk to me. Other colleagues stopped attending meetings if I were present. The impact of these behaviors falls far below the impact of the words describing them. One colleague began a whisper campaign, saying that my tenure "would lower the bar" of tenure overall and that it would be to the detriment of the school if I were to receive it. Another colleague said to me that strings were being pulled for me and questioned, directly to me, "Why would you want them to give you tenure just because you are disabled?" And another colleague tried time and time again to stop my tenure process from moving forward through repeated meetings with the school administration—knowing full well what this would mean for me, for my career, and for my quality of life. I do not mean to suggest that these sentiments were pervasive, as I am also surrounded by colleagues who are caring and compassionate and supportive, but they were present. And they were destructive. And I faced them day after day. I went to work knowing I would be surrounded by people with these beliefs and left work, more often than not, in tears.

This is the other form of infantilization of people with disabilities. This is the form that is based in malice or repugnance and not simply in misunderstanding. It is the argument that an individual with a disability is inferior, less capable, less deserving simply by virtue of her disability. It is the diminishing of respect for the accomplishments of an individual with disability, under the assumption that these accomplishments were somehow favors or gifts or not held to the same standard as everyone else's. It is the minimization and infantilization of the contributions that people with disabilities make because doing so better fits into our narrative of them. It is using a perceived incapability as the basis for marginalization and omission.

This was not the first time I had encountered this form of infantilization—this form of prejudice—but it was the most protracted, the most unrelenting, the most hurtful, and the most surprising. People with disabilities confront these types of beliefs every day. As a result, we are left behind in the workforce and society, in general. The belief that people with disabilities are less able is used to justify the innate bigotry and discomfort that other people have toward them. It provides the reason for their marginalization—they are simply unfit for the position, they are ill-equipped for what they need to do, they are not as talented as anyone else, they are getting something that they did not deserve—and, thus, they are reduced to insignificance.

I am seen as a disabled person before I am seen as anything else—before I am seen as a colleague or a researcher or a human being. I understand that, but I have lived my life trying to change that. The presence of my disability and my life as a person living with it, that is not who I am. I am not my disability, and I choose not to adhere to the invisibility that my disability can create. And because of this invisibility, many people know far less about me than I would like them to. So, this is what I want people to know about me. . . .

Like so many other authors, David Foster Wallace was just as much—and possibly more—a philosophical thinker as he was an author. You can't reasonably expect to effectively capture the human experience in a narrative without also thinking about why people do what they do or what values guide their decision-making. Wallace knew this and explored the complexity of humanity as well as anyone.

In one of the interviews Wallace gave before he took his life in 2008, he discussed with gut-wrenching honesty his fears, concerns, and observations of the state of humanity in general and American culture in specific. In the interview, which lasted over ninety minutes, Wallace spoke about the distinction between the things we want and the things we need, and how distinguishing between these two categories can be among the most difficult yet important work that we have to undertake throughout our lives. I struggle with this distinction every day.

When you live with quadriplegia, the list of things you need becomes simultaneously minimalist and maximized. When you live with quadriplegia, you learn very quickly that many of the things you thought you could never live without, you, in fact, can. But also, the fragility of life can make us reliant on unexpected things. When you live with quadriplegia, you become keenly aware of the things you need—access to medical care, assistance in daily necessities like eating, bathing, going to the bathroom. Pursuing these things speaks to our intrinsic humanness but also to how the world denies dignity to those who require assistance in their pursuit. We are unified in our need to fill or empty our bladders and bowels but ostracized for needing assistance to do it. We are unified in our need for sustenance but infantilized if we can't gain access to this sustenance on our own. When you live with quadriplegia, the pressing nature of these needs becomes much more acute, that much more real yet vulnerable.

My needs—not "special needs" but human needs—have been stripped to life's essentials. I need help accessing that which I need, so the list is, by necessity and practicality, truncated to the barest of barest essentials. It's perhaps utterly unsurprising that the Spartan truncation of my needs has led to a Caligulan expansion of my wants. Many of the things I thought I needed have been reprioritized and demoted, and my wants are now plentiful.

I want to stretch the next time I yawn. I want to take a deep breath of the precise volume of my choosing, and then hold the air in my lungs for the duration I desire. I want to spend one day, or even one hour, or even one minute without focusing on when my next breath will come and being intensely aware if it arrives even a fraction of a second late. I want to brush my own hair and my own teeth, applying to each an amount of pressure or resistance that is required to produce the bit of pain that lets you know you've done an adequate job. I want to take a shower without the observation of anyone else and to feel the warmth of the water running over my body. I want to masturbate. I want to turn my head from side to side to greet someone as he walks into the room. I want to scratch an itch without asking and waiting for help. I want to live an entire day without thinking about when my blood pressure might deviate wildly from normal. I want to live an entire day without my muscles spasming against me. I want to touch all of the scars on my body and appraise them for the stories they tell.

I want to have gone to work by myself, driving my own car there and back, only to come home and flop on the couch in exaggerated exhaustion. I want to go grocery shopping and squeeze the oranges for freshness. I want to leave my house spontaneously, without having to think about when my lungs were most recently suctioned, and go anyplace without having to be concerned about what inaccessibility impediments lie on the other end. I want to go for a long walk in the woods or up the side of the mountain until my legs ache with hard-earned fatigue. I want to run across a field and lie in the grass, wrapping my fingers around individual blades like they were woven into me.

I want to dance, my God, how I want to dance—slow and fast, by myself and with someone I love. I want to play every favorite song I have had over the past thirty years and feel the sense of abandon that is only brought about when you completely let go of yourself. I want to drink too much and sleep until the next afternoon without thinking about how this would affect a schedule or alter a regimented life. I want to sleep on a friend's floor. I want to sleep on the beach in the sun and cool off in the ocean.

I want to hug all of the people I love—to wrap my arms around them and not let go, even after a socially acceptable amount of time has passed.

I want to hold my nephews' hands, tickle their legs, and play with them on the floor. I want to make dinner for my family—all of their favorite foods—and clean up afterward.

I want to travel. I want to see parts of the world I've only read about or seen pictures of—to travel in person rather than by proxy. I want to drive cross-country, only stopping when I need to sleep, and eat at dive joints that only the locals know and treasure. I want to immerse myself completely in a culture other than my own. I want to go to the top of the Eiffel Tower and look at the lights of Paris at midnight. I want to visit a village in Africa and learn true wisdom from the people there.

I want to live in a world that does not evaluate my worth as a human being based on an arbitrary and socially constructed definition of normal. I want to live in a world in which physical ability is not eroded by ill-informed policy decisions that prioritize barriers over inclusion. I want to see people with disabilities in every social circle, in every stratum of society, embodying every kind of leadership role and position of power that is afforded to anyone else. I want to never know what it means to be excluded, and I want no one else to have to know either.

There was a time in my life when the line between the things I wanted and the things I needed was far blurrier and more membrane-like. There was a time when I didn't understand that the things so many of us do reflexively and without a second's thought—as if they are a guaranteed part of human existence—are in no way guaranteed. My rearrangement of wants and needs, like rearrangements of assets and liabilities on a balance sheet, has allowed me to better understand the true value in my life. It has given me the vision and hard-earned wisdom to appreciate the things that I have intrinsically and will never lose, and those things that I long for but have learned are possible to live without.

5

←——————→

BOTH WAYS

The reality we observe is a product of the perspective we take. In our lives, especially those stricken by trauma or catastrophe, we need to look both ways.

I OWN A CONDOMINIUM ON the East End of Long Island. It's a little sanctuary I bought for myself, close enough to my home in Stony Brook but, at the same time, far enough away to feel like going there is wholly different from being home. That was really my motivation for purchasing this condo. For my parents and me, taking trips and vacations is difficult and possibly more stressful than it is worth. But I wanted a place where my family and I could go that was equipped for my needs, a place where we could go to relax and escape some of the demands of our daily lives.

My little refuge sits on Long Island's North Shore overlooking the Long Island Sound. On a clear day, you can see all the way to the shores of

Connecticut, and on a less clear day, you can see sunsets that incorporate every color to be found on a painter's palette. It is a small piece of what I expect anyone's heuristic of heaven might be: a little place of solace.

Throughout the spring and fall, I try to go out to the condo as frequently as my schedule allows. In the spring, there are strawberry festivals and outdoor fairs, and in the autumn, there are pumpkin festivals and holiday festivities of all different kinds. This is a haven of Long Island that, although it is gaining popularity among New York City getaway seekers, has managed to keep its slow pace and rural charm. Especially over recent years, this slow pace has been restorative and rejuvenating for me when times have required some restoration and rejuvenation.

I also saw this place as a location to build traditions and memories with my nephews, Carter, Jamie, Harrison, Ollie, and Teddy. My sister, brother, and I have memories of taking day trips to the East End as children, going pumpkin and apple picking in the fields owned by Long Island farmers. I wanted the same memories for my nephews—memories that they could build their identities and lives upon, visions of their past that would help to define who they are, where they came from, and where they are headed. I want them to associate their childhoods with the serenity and tranquility that this place encapsulates, and I want it to be how they understand themselves.

There is an expansive, lush green lawn that separates two of the complex buildings, right before the bluff leading down to the water. The lawn is frequented by a steady rotation of renters who come to stay for a holiday weekend or as guests for a wedding at one of the nearby vineyards. Families, often young and happy to be outside the confines of the city, set up blankets and tents on the lawn like campers, watching the small waves come to the shore. Groomsmen and bachelor-party-goers throw baseballs and frisbees across the lawn like it is a return to a childhood playground.

When I go out east for the weekend or for the day, I sit on the deck that overlooks both the lawn and the sound beyond it. I can see sailboats in the distance, likely carrying Nutmeggers or residents from Block Island, making their way west toward Manhattan and the adjacent suburbs. And I can see the guests on the lawn, often close enough to make eye contact, as they play or eat or drink under the sun. It is a place where I can go to think and reflect on my life—looking both to the field, teeming with vitality, and looking to the sea, the vision of tranquility and serenity. They are two contiguous aspects of the same picture, each representing a part of the whole that is different yet no less picturesque than the other. It is to me, at least to some small degree, what I expect Key West was to Hemingway or what Lake Garda was to Proust: a place of solace but not solitude, a place of introspection but not introversion. Thirty years of life with quadriplegia leaves you with many intricacies of life to sort out and many angles from which to view them.

My disability has given me moments of inconsolable sadness, forcing me to grieve ideas of what would have been or sometimes even should have been. Living with quadriplegia has driven me to times of immeasurable frustration, yearning for memories of touch and possibilities of movement. My paralysis has caused circumstances of intense fear, making me curse the fragility that life sometimes forces us to realize. Living life in a wheelchair has subjected me to instances of subjugation and marginalization, leading me to believe, falsely but insidiously, that my value or worth were a function of my virility rather than my virtue. These moments of sadness, frustration, fear, and subjugation could easily have seemed like the most prominent features if I looked at my life in only one way. But as any great artist could attest, the reality we observe is a product of the perspective we take. In our lives, especially those stricken by trauma or catastrophe, we need to look both ways.

My disability has given me both a framework and a lens to view the world. The parts of life that are difficult can teach you valuable lessons about who you are and the strength you have, and these can become inseparable from the vantage point from which the world is seen. Times of difficulty imply sadness, frustration, and fear, and only the most thrill-seeking or noblest among us would freely and willingly subject ourselves to intense difficulty. But the human brain, the human heart, and the human spirit embody the antidotes to all of these, and in measures that we often cannot predict. That is the fulcrum that balances our lives. That is the panopticon that provides a more complete view of a vision that could otherwise be looked at from only one way.

I have lived my life from the vantage point of nondisabled and disabled. Age difference notwithstanding, thirty years later, I can better appreciate the resolution of images seen from one perspective as opposed to another. My disability has forced me to be patient and, in those times of patience, to be more aware of both the passage of time and beauty in it. The fragility of my life has forced me to be earnest in the things I want to do, and more mindful of the limited energy I have to do them. Like the absence of light that is required to ultimately see the images of a photograph developed in a darkroom, there is a clarity of detail that begins to develop when difficulty is central to how you understand your life. A life lived with extreme challenge can illuminate that which may have been obscured; a life lived with extreme difficulty can better identify and contextualize others of its kind, seeing it as a common bond of strength and perseverance, and you gravitate toward it, knowing that it has immense weight.

I receive a great deal of email from people all over the world, and in the waning months of 2020, I received an email from a young boy, Connor Berryhill, who was diagnosed with autism spectrum disorder. Rarely, if ever, have I received an email that touched me as deeply or inspired me as much as Connor's did. Only a child, Connor had already written an autobiography and had founded a nonprofit organization. Yet age has never been a fair measure of wisdom, and Connor was able to put into words that which, in my forty-plus years, I have not been able to. He wrote to me, in ideas that laid the foundation for his second book, how he views his—and in fact all—disability as a form of superheroism. As I told Connor in my response, our thinking is quite closely aligned, though Connor reached his understanding much sooner in his life than I had in mine.

I am a woman with a disability. I am a disabled woman. These are two statements that I make with pride. Unexpectedly enormous pride. To some, myself included at one point in my life, the qualifier "disabled" connotes some inferior or unfortunate status, the modifier that demotes by its very existence. By the word's very construction, starting with a negatively oriented prefix, we are led to believe this. People from all corners of the world become the thinkers and speakers of an ideology and a vernacular that often knows nothing about the lens that disability—or difficulty of any kind—puts on your perspective. It is not the sadness or frustration or fear or subjugation that comes to define who you are, it is the way your identity assumes these factors and then keeps going that defines who you are. You encounter struggle, but you can learn to overtake that struggle with adaptation and creativity, and then you never look at struggle in the same way again. You encounter frustration, but you learn to subsume that frustration with patience and acceptance, and then sources of frustration begin to seem feeble, commonplace, and impotent. You face times of sadness, but you learn that those can be squelched by friendship and love, and then those two virtues become unconquerable. And you are tested by fear, but you learn to erase it through hope, until hope becomes the cornerstone on which you live your life. Over time, you begin to learn that it is not the sadness or frustration or fear or struggle that sets your identity any more than "dis" circumscribes your ability. It is the opposite of each of these—which we must have in unusual, or as some might say, *superhero* amounts—that defines you. And if those characteristics are not the very characteristics which we, as a society, find most valuable and in which we ought to take most pride, then I have miscalculated some of the most precious parts of my existence.

Sitting on the deck outside of my condominium, I have had the opportunity to think about my life, my identity, and how people view me. I have been told that when people tell you something about yourself, you should listen, as it might teach you something you didn't fully appreciate before. So, sitting on the deck, watching the sun shimmer on the water, I try to take the time to think about some of these visions or versions of myself. I have been called *hypersensitive*, a term whose definition has always eluded me and seems somewhat ironic for someone experiencing sensory loss. Is it possible to feel too much or too deeply? I suppose, as with any characteristic, there is a normal distribution surrounding *sensitivity*, or how much one emotionally responds to circumstances. If that's the case, in fairness, I also suppose that I should position myself on the uppermost extremes of that distribution. I cry easily at movies, music, or world events. I am easily hurt by the people I love, not always because they have done something worthy of that hurt but because I feel it, nonetheless. I feel enraged by circumstances of injustice and, when I believe injustice is directed to me, I can feel as though the world I have striven to remain a part of wants me less than I want it. I startle with little provocation, clench my teeth with fury until they chip, and can be so overcome by the burdens of stress or exhaustion that either fits of tears or bursts of laughter are the only way to alleviate them.

So, yes, I might be "hypersensitive," and according to those who know me, I have been this way all my life. But when you live with quadriplegia or, I would suspect, other disabilities, your ability to release the pent-up emotion brought about by daily stressors or excitement in life is substantially reduced. When faced with times of frustration or anger, I am not able to just go for a run or take a drive alone to clear my head. When encountering moments of exhilaration, I have not had the luxury of screaming or jumping with joy, running in circles until I am ready to fall down. Instead, all of these emotions stay trapped like captives in the walls of my chest, in the confines of my mind, until they find their escape route.

But as Newton's third law would predict, there is an equal and opposite force to balance the feelings of sensitivity I have in my own life. Disability and trauma have the potential to make one that much more aware of the severity of the pain and struggle that others encounter in their lives. I can understand the instances in life that tear your heart out and then our often-maladroit attempts to fit it back in, and I understand them because I have lived that very same extraction and ham-handedness. Having undergone trauma makes it that much more evident in the lives of those around you, like a hand reaching out to grab on to that of another. And, interestingly, you come to realize that there are many out there to reach. Given the extremity of the experiences that my family and I have undergone, it would be easy to think that many people might be reluctant to share the intricacies and intimacy of their own difficult experiences with us, as if incomparable suffering creates a barrier to communication. However, much the opposite is the case, and thankfully so.

The trauma and challenges that my family and I have undergone are blatant and well-known. People look at us with the understanding that we have been through—and, more importantly, lived through—an event or series of battles that have been unimaginably difficult. In that understanding, they find an ally. They find another member of life's blessed union of souls beleaguered by unexpected and more expected pitfalls, another heart that has been forced to feel more emotion than the amount for which it is designed. There is an invisible yet powerful bond to be found in that realization, an understanding that, while we can suffer individually, none of us suffers alone.

I use the word "suffer" for its ease and clarity, but I do that knowing it is not quite accurate and requires much more nuance. Suffering is a time-bound concept: the depths of the emotion that we feel when the acuity of trauma is highest and we are left bereft. But you can't suffer forever, and the termination of that time-bound experience is usually either self-inflicted or self-actualized. Suffering begets struggle. However, struggle bears little resemblance to its predecessor. Struggle is an action-oriented idea that, by its very nature, strives for something better. We don't struggle toward reaching a worse outcome, though we might suffer until we reach one. We struggle to reach our next safe harbor, point of equilibrium, new way of understanding our lives. We struggle to reach the end of our pain. We struggle to find ways to grapple with realities we may never have had before. We struggle to understand the image of our lives when seemingly unbearable holes have been created in it. But throughout all of these, we are willing ourselves to some better state.

I have suffered, suffered in ways that I never knew humans could suffer. There have been times when I have lost myself in this suffering, feeling unmoored in a miasma of pain and uncertainty. And the labyrinth of unanswered questions and miscalculated outcomes was terrifying. But there is a pristine point when the disorientation of suffering begins to take a form; a structure, however complicated and fraught with impediments, presents itself. I have struggled, and not always successfully, to visualize the structure in suffering and navigate it. But what the purveyors of struggle—in whatever form that struggle might take—never reveal is that struggle has its own progeny. Struggle demands and begets adaptation and creativity. Creativity and adaptation also bear little resemblance to their predecessor. While also action-oriented ideas that strive for something better, creativity and adaptation allow us to see with much higher resolution what we need to do, how we need to change, and the realities we need to embrace or reject in order to live. We don't adapt or become creative so that we are experiencing a worse condition, though we might struggle through these. We adapt and create so that the realities we are facing are, once again, livable. We adapt and create so that circumstances we had never envisioned for our lives or thought we might be able to tolerate become habitual. And throughout all of these, we become stronger by virtue of our challenge, not weaker from it.

Adaptability and creativity know no boundaries of problem type. Adaptability and creativity are self-perpetuating concepts that bore themselves deeply into a way of life, allowing us to become more able to grapple with any number of oddities or unfortunate experiences that life inevitably and unrelentingly waylays us with. Adaptation and creativity are needs-based characteristics which don't often present themselves unless asked for or demanded from us—any of us. But at the same time, they are nondiscriminatory in their integration into parts of our lives that far exceed their origin.

My family and I have adapted to life with disability. We have become creative in how we handle the routine impediments that life continues to challenge us with and have adapted to a way of life that few others can imagine. Yet, at the same time, the shoulders on which we balance other challenging circumstances in our lives have broadened. When you have seen life at its most difficult and its darkest, there are few other challenges that look so menacing. When you have become accustomed to difficulty, the jagged edges of it become worn down.

There is, unquestionably, immeasurable amounts of frustration that accompany a life of difficulty, whatever form that difficulty might take. While you can adapt and be creative, there is a frustration that you ever had to be adaptive to begin with: a feeling of unfairness or resentment that the maze you have found yourself in is not the maze that others have to navigate. It is easy to become disenchanted by all the big, and even all the less significant, ways that life appears to be punitive; these, unfortunately, don't ever go away. Sometimes they are fewer in number or smaller in size, but they don't ever really go away. And they don't go away because they are endemic to everyone. Difficulty and heartache are a systematic part of the human experience, the unsigned guarantee that we all make upon entering the world.

Repeatedly experiencing disability or trauma or difficulty of any kind does not make you immune to instances of frustration. Indeed, experiencing disability or trauma or difficulty asymptotically increases your encounters with frustration to what seems like a limitless extent. The number of times that I complain of frustration—frustration with how circumstances are unfolding or with the trials I have to undergo every day—is enormous. But frustration is an emotion that, in and of itself, has no prescribed outcome. No amount of frustration is going to yield a desired end. Being frustrated has no effect on the quality or speed of a resolution, and it is in many ways functionless—with the exception that it is a valuable educator on patience.

Because frustration does not yield a resolution, it forces one to learn to endure, to accept, and to be patient. If I stopped being frustrated only after the source of my frustration was resolved, I would never *not* be frustrated. I have been frustrated by my inability to walk, breathe, embrace, and move, and those frustrations have not been resolved, so I've learned to endure them. I've learned to be patient while I wait for things I know might not come. I have been frustrated by manifestations of ignorance and outright bigotry, but I have learned to endure them. I've learned to be patient while finding ways to change them. I have been frustrated by bureaucratic unwillingness—by insurance companies, home health-care providers, municipalities—to make common sense decisions that can increase quality of life, but I've learned to endure it, to be patient while fighting to make change. And I have been frustrated by how much longer it takes and how much more difficult it is to deal with the very basic necessities of life, each and every day, and how that robs me of time to do so many other things that I would enjoy or find meaning in, but I've learned to endure this. I've learned to be patient while doing what needs to be done.

Sensitivity, adaptability, creativity, endurance, patience. These are the corollaries that have, for me, sat alongside the evolution of my life with a disability. Are they superpowers? Well, there isn't anything that is particularly "super" about them, at least not in the sense that they are unique or exclusive to people who have undergone disability or trauma. However, in order to live each day with the demands that disability and trauma can put on your life, these qualities—these virtues that are the makings of superheroes—are needed in abundance. These qualities become the basis of your identity.

My disability is part of my identity. But what does that mean, exactly?

We talk about matters like "identity" and "identity politics" in our discourse quite frivolously, and these ideas are sometimes scoffed at, as if they are inconsequential to who we are as people, individually and collectively. Those who dismiss identity, or how we choose to define ourselves, speak from an inherently privileged place: a privilege that comes from being defined by society in the very way you choose to define yourself. As a matter of fact, there was a prolonged period of time in which the self-designation of identity was unimaginable, when identity was virtually assigned to someone and not the product of how we choose to understand ourselves. We are fortunate enough now to live in a time when, at least for some people in some places, there is liberality with respect to how we understand ourselves and that that understanding does not have to be identical to how we are reflexively seen by others.

I completed my PhD at Stony Brook University in the field of sociology and science policy. Within sociological circles, the concept of identity is vigorously debated and hotly pursued, as people—academics and nonacademics alike—are always looking for ways to better understand themselves. We are often far better at thinking we understand someone else than we are at attempting to understand ourselves, and so often we look to divining rods or Rosetta stones to decode that which is completely within our grasp to understand. In response to this, many sociological thinkers have tackled the issue of identity—what it means, how we develop it, in what context it applies versus when it does not apply. There are some sociological thinkers who have argued that our identities are the product of meanings we develop through our interaction with other people in specific environments. Our identity puts us in a specific social structure because of the relationships that an identity can imply, and they become symbols that can vary across time, situation, and people involved. People can develop an identity construction for someone else based on a mental negotiation process that involves the creation of social constructions and interactions. Identities, then, are the product of our conversations with other people and what we learn about them by interacting with them. We can "identify" aspects of someone's physical composition but can only understand a true "identity" through a process that goes much deeper, looks more discerningly, is built on common exchanges.

But what if you don't take the time to have those interactions or make those negotiations? If you fail to take the time required to know someone, on what can you legitimately base your assessment? People with disabilities face this conundrum all the time. Especially when they are spotted "in the wild"—the places that people typically go when living life—people with disabilities are evaluated and judged by some schema that others have created about what disability entails and what basic dignity should be afforded to them. That is to say, people with disabilities are often evaluated and judged by a social construct and idea that places them at the margins—those not to be included and those whose lives we would rather not know about.

The idea of disability intrinsically makes people uncomfortable. I know it, I understand it, and I have experienced it. We perceive an unwellness or a lack of wholeness that we don't want to either associate with or be reminded of. So when I sit on my patio on the East End of Long Island, that might be the understanding that people—without any conversation or context—gain and the identity they perceive: someone who is unwell or not complete. It is easy to cast aside someone who we believe to be less than everyone else. I have experienced this phenomenon—this stigma—as a person with a disability, and I have participated in this as a person without a disability.

The concept of "stigma" as it relates to a person's identity was first discussed by the iconic sociologist Erving Goffman. Essentially what Goffman argued was that stigma was a product of the socially constructed nature of identity, in which an individual is "disqualified" from full social acceptance. The word "stigma" comes from the ancient Greeks to refer to signs designed to expose something fundamentally flawed about the moral status of the individual to whom we attach the stigma. In the time of the ancient Greeks, demarcations were literally carved or beaten into the body of an individual, such as a slave, criminal, or traitor, to put on display their shame and ostracization. Though the implications of this term have evolved over the centuries, today it's used in a manner similar to its original sense: as a reference to aspects of oneself worthy of disgrace. But throughout many years of sociological history, there wasn't much attention given to the social structures that influence our thoughts, shape our actions, and work to create stigma.

It is entirely society's creation that dictates how we categorize people and what attributes we ascribe to them. A stigma puts the individual into a category, or her social identity, so that we have more attributes to ascribe to an individual above and beyond things like social status or position in the world. Now, the utilization of stigmas often takes place unconsciously. Stigmas lay the groundwork for many of the biases that we develop about people. Stigmas help to form the ideas that society, collectively, has constructed and, as a result, things that we have come to believe. But as Goffman wrote, "Typically, we do not become aware that we have made these demands or aware of what they are until an active question arises as to whether or not they will be fulfilled. It is then that we are likely to realize that all along we had been making certain assumptions as to what the individual before us ought to be."[9] Goffman went on to write:

> While the stranger is present before us, evidence can arise of his possessing an attribute that makes him different from others in the category of persons available for him to be, and of a less desirable kind—in the extreme, a person who is quite thoroughly bad or dangerous or

weak. He is thus reduced in our minds from a whole and unusual person to a tainted, discounted one. Such an attribute is a stigma, especially when its discrediting effect is very extensive; sometimes it is also called a failing, a shortcoming, a handicap. It constitutes a special discrepancy between virtual and actual social identity.[10]

On paper, the ideas of "stigma" and the writings of Erving Goffman might appear much less revelatory to the nonsociologist than to the sociologist. However, in actuality, this man and his ideas have significant relevance to our daily interactions and who we choose to include in our conversations or social circles. Historically speaking, stigmatized individuals, those we have socially constructed to be different from, inferior to, or less than the generalized population, have been systematically excluded from conversations and decisions that directly affect their lives, as well as from opportunities to participate in the same way that others do. People with disabilities, thought to be the weak or vulnerable, are primary among these groups.

In the United States, people with disabilities are far from the first or only group who have had to associate their identities with a stigmatized idea or social construct. Black and Brown Americans, LGBTQ individuals, members of sexual minorities, immigrants, veterans—all of these people have had their identities linked to social constructs and stereotypes that have attempted to place them on a lower rung of the social hierarchy in the very same way that people with disabilities have been. The internal mental negotiation pairs these groups with negative ideas that society has unfairly created about them, attempting to place them in a denigrated or socially inferior position. We are all familiar with some of the negative ideas that we have created pertaining to diverse groups—stereotypes that produce biases, biases that shape perception. I choose not to discuss these so as to not perpetuate them.

But when it comes to disability, there are some additionally complicating factors that further marginalize those individuals from those who create opinions about them. For many demographic groups, membership is largely immutable and more intrinsic than inclusion among people with disabilities is. You either are a member of a particular racial group or you are not. You either have arrived as an immigrant from another country or you haven't. The inclusion lines of disability are more malleable and porous than other groups, and when you have stigma in conjunction with the lingering potentiality of unwittingly becoming included in the group with that stigma, you want to keep it as far away from you as possible.

Many people with disabilities—and rightly so—are proud of their identity as disabled. Many people with disabilities find companionship and tight social networks among others with disability; they are activists, lobbyists, artists, and change makers of immense talent, and they fill these roles and form these relationships not despite their disability but often because of their disability. Disability is a part of who they are, not a source of shame or embarrassment or something to "get over," but a vital and important part of how they understand themselves. For these people, the stigma associated with disability is, instead, a mobilizing source of pride and self-worth. I count myself among these people. But not everyone feels the same way.

For many people who live with disability, *disabled* was not their native identity. For many, a life with disability was the result of a regrettable accident, injury, or disease that is associated with trauma, pain, and limitation. The mobilization around understanding disability as a source of pride, then, is much harder to achieve. A disability can become a physical representation of that which we regret ever having happened, or a reminder of that which was once possible but is no longer so, or the manifestation of an identity or stereotype that we, ourselves, were once uncomfortable with. For these people, the stigma associated with disability can be rebelled against and something that causes more regret than pride. I count myself among these people, as well.

These two ways of looking at disability as an identity are opposing but not at all mutually exclusive. In an unironic way, it is entirely possible to be intensely proud of life as a disabled person but, at the same time, want to enjoy the benefits that are afforded to most everyone else. It is entirely possible to take pride in disability as an aspect of who you are and how you live your life but, at the same time, not want to endure the indignities, frustration, and pain that disability can produce. It is entirely possible to feel one way about yourself on one day and entirely differently about yourself on another. There is nothing wrong with that. There is nothing to be ashamed of about that. Everyone grapples with the intensity of disability in different ways and at different times, and understanding disability as a virtuous part of identity is an evolutionary process that waxes and wanes depending on a host of factors. Undeniably, unquestionably, without a moment's hesitation, one of the most central among these factors that influence how someone living with disability understands herself on any given day is the result of the society that welcomes her into it, the society that treats her like a valued member of it, the community that wants him there just as much as he wants to be there, the community that would operate less well in his absence, the world that says we want you to be a part of us and see you for the humanity, sensitivity, strength, creativity, and hope that you bring.

I have often thought about conducting a thought experiment, asking people how they would feel if they were told today that they would be disabled tomorrow. I have often thought about what people might fear most about the prospects of this happening. Would it be the uncertainty of having to adjust to a life lived with disability, and all the adjustments and planning that would have to be made to accommodate the disabled life? Would it be a loss of independence—that many more activities of daily life would have to be conducted with some assistance? Would it be the expected loss of or inability to find a romantic relationship—that the reach of love finds its limits where and when disability begins? Would it be the perceived hardship that is associated with living with a disability—the barriers that disability presents in going about daily life? Would it be the presumed inability to enjoy the things you had enjoyed—travel, sports, driving, sex? Or would it be the expected marginalization and lack of social participation that disability produces—that being disabled puts you on the sidelines or inside the house, in a separate class from those you are familiar with? After experiencing disability, all of these outcomes are possibilities, but they are far from certainties. And they are possibilities because we, as a society, have chosen to make them possibilities.

The year I graduated from Harvard, the commencement speaker was economist Amartya Sen. Looking back some twenty years later, I wish I had known more about Sen's work and the significance of the contributions he has made to intellectual thought of all kinds, because I would have paid closer attention to the words and ideas of this man, this Nobel laureate, this true luminary. Working with his colleague, Martha Nussbaum, Sen crafted what is known as the "capability approach"[11] as a new way of researching, talking about, and then ultimately maximizing human well-being. The capability approach involves three things: capabilities, freedoms, and functionings, which, though they sound similar, refer to different ideas related to overall quality of life. To put this theory in its most elemental and understandable form, capabilities are freedoms to do and be various things, like participate in society or live to an old age. The things in our lives that we want to do and want to be, the things that capabilities are built on, according to this theory, are functionings—things like being healthy, having a job, having respect, having enough to eat. So, for instance, if I wanted the capability of participating actively in changing the world for the better, it would rely on functionings like going to school, getting an education, having a job, living in a supportive community. It is very difficult to achieve the capabilities we want without the functionings to get there. But there are aspects of life that reduce our capabilities, or reduce our ability to achieve the life we want. Poverty is one, since a lack of resources reduces the ways people can be nourished, educated, or take part in the community. Disability is another aspect of life that reduces our capabilities or the paths we have to live a rich and meaningful life.

Partially in response to this work, in 2001, the World Health Organization developed what's called the International Classification of Functioning, Disability, and Health, or ICF, model.[12] The purpose of this model is to provide a common language for health and health-related states—language that everyone could use—to enhance the policies and social services that impact people's lives. The ICF model essentially states that everyone, whether or not they are "disabled," has some level of physical ability, and that "disability" is not simply a binary category of belonging to or not. Our level of ability impacts our functioning, but our functioning is also impacted by all sorts of environmental factors and participation barriers that affect how we live our lives, what we do, who we are, and who we become.

The ICF model is biopsychosocial and, as a result, a fairly comprehensive view of disability. It doesn't understand disability to be a medical or health-related issue alone, but a product of physical ability, social attitudes, climate, geography, matters of public policy, and supports of people around us. This is revolutionary thinking, though in actuality it shouldn't be. The intuition and logic are fairly simple: We all have some level of physical ability, which changes throughout our lives—sometimes we need assistance; at some point in our lives we might need glasses or hearing aids; at another point in our lives we might be diagnosed with MS. But our ability to achieve the things we want to in life is not just a function of this—it is a product of the policies that give us opportunities. It's a product of the social supports that allow us to thrive. It's a product of technology that is made available to us. It's a product of the attitudes and levels of discrimination that either facilitate or stifle the feelings of empowerment that we have about ourselves. All of these things are con-tributors to disability, or to ability, and many of them can be addressed if we decide to address them.

This is where many people within the disability community sit on the issue of disability and its effects on people's lives. Living with a disability is a part of one's identity of which anyone ought to be proud. Though many people with a disability might prefer to live without it, it is the social narrative regarding disability that needs to change so that the physical part of disability is not considered to be a source of shame or inadequacy. This part is entirely socially constructed, and it needs to be deconstructed and then reconstructed. I am immensely proud of the life I have led and the person I have become purely because of my disability, and for anyone who fails to see this, the loss is on them. However, at the same time, there are undoubtedly social deficits that I experience because of this same dis-ability that I often wish I did not have to encounter.

It is these social deficits that I believe people fear when they envision the prospects of becoming disabled. You can learn to not simply live but thrive with a physical disability. It might be only a few people's decidedly chosen life, but it is a valuable life. A purposeful life. A life that generates vast sums of the virtues we wish to see in ourselves but often only see in other people. It is the social deficits that can be much more difficult to grapple with, especially because they are out of one's own hands to fix and because they are so seemingly unnecessary if we only took the time to work on them.

My biggest fear, after learning what quadriplegia was and how it would affect my life, was not the prospect of living with paralysis in itself, although that was frightening because of its unfamiliarity. My biggest fear was that I wouldn't be able to be surrounded by my friends, that access to the school system that I had always known and that was essential to my future would be denied from me. It should not have taken the fight that it required to ensure that my attendance in school would be possible, but were it not for that possibility and that aspect of childhood normality, the detour that my life had taken might have been too much to bear.

In the years that have passed since, it has almost always been the avoidable, socially constructed, and antiquated societal barriers that have been the greatest source of frustration and sadness. I lived with and feared the sense of isolation that disability might create, not due to the disability itself, but because the notion of inclusion did not, and still does not, extend to people with disabilities. Upon graduating from Harvard, an institution that, for many, bestows an enormous opportunity and privilege, I feared the inability to find any appropriate employment whatsoever. I knew what my talents were, how my commitment to hard work and perseverance were deeply integrated into my way of life, but I believed that those typically sought-after characteristics would fall far below the salience of my physical state. I have feared what might become of my life and how my future might continue to develop if and when something happens to the people who care for me. I have feared a future spent in a medical institution—far from the academic institutions that have characterized my life—and how long I could possibly survive there. I have mourned what I thought to be an inescapable inability to find love as well as the absence of happiness that that elusive relationship would create. I feared a hollowness at the core of my being that would never be filled by the companionship of another and how that emptiness might leave me embittered or resentful. I feared all of these things, yes, but I cursed them at the same time, as their solutions seemed simple, but beyond my own, isolated sphere of influence.

Addressing the fears that I, like many others, have encountered throughout a life with disability might be beyond any one person's individual sphere of influence, but it is well within a collective sphere of influence. This is where the social construct part of disability makes itself obvious. It should not be taken as given that a person with a disability ought to fear unemployment despite his talents, because we can craft policies to incentivize his hiring and his full productivity so everyone is better off. It should not be assumed that a person with a disability must experience isolation or structural marginalization, because efforts to mainstream disabled children into the classroom should be everyone's goal, not simply that of weary parents, and this should be so much the case that marginalization and exclusion are simply unthinkable. And fears of loneliness or lovelessness should not be the assumption of any disabled person, because we can demand that our culture changes the way it represents their beauty, sexuality, worth, and humanity.

But we haven't done this yet. Our society has not moved itself far enough forward yet. We see only the land or only the water and fail to see all of the gradients by which one transforms into the other or the beauty in capturing the whole scene. I would not be who I am were it not for my disability and all of the struggles it has presented. I would not be who I am were it not for my disability and all of the understandings it has given me. I could never exchange one for the other, nor would I want to. I am a disabled woman, both humbly and proudly, embodying all of the vulnerabilities but also all of the strength that this identity precipitates. For me, one cannot exist without the other, but I had to look in both directions in order to understand that.

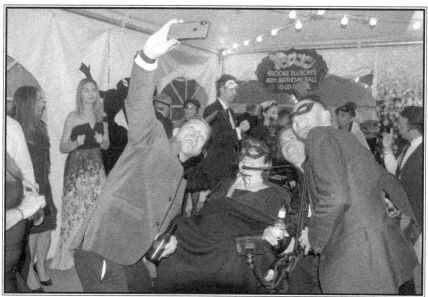

*Brooke celebrating with friends and guests at her fortieth birthday
masquerade ball, October 20, 2018.*

6

I LOVE

The fact of the matter is that my life story is a love story.

I HAVE BEEN IN LOVE once in my life. I don't think I knew it at the time, and I only know it now by looking at it in retrospect. Maybe I didn't know what I was supposed to feel; maybe I had a different expectation of what it was supposed to look like; or maybe I had a different vision of who I would fall in love with. But I was in love once in my life.

What more is there to be said about love that has not already been said by someone more qualified than I am to say it? Well, love and disability are two topics that are too rarely talked about together. It's almost as if one of these concepts cannot simultaneously exist in the presence of the other—as though disability, especially wheelchair use, takes place on a plane that knows nothing of fundamental human emotions like love. Any wheelchair user would tell you that that isn't true.

Though I've been in love once in my life, I have been in many—far too many—relationships that were loving and could very well have been love. Who really knows what love is or what its requisite defining characteristics are? None of us is given instruction because there is no instruction manual for love. But many of the relationships that I have had have embodied all of the things that I have ever thought love would constitute.

My relationships with people are close and intense. My relationships have a heaviness to them, on which I pride myself but over which I have little control. The depth of my experiences in life forces me to want to interact with people deeply and personally. I have little time, and far less energy, for things without substance. That belief is carried through in relationships I hold and friendships I make.

Romantic relationships are fundamentally difficult, for everyone, but significantly more so when you have a disability. But not for reasons that you would expect. I think there is a presupposition held by many that I simply can't be in a romantic relationship or that people with disabilities ought not to be longing for that. There is a presupposition that there is no crossover in intimacy or love between people who are disabled and those who are not. It is understood as if there were an implicit taboo or barrier that everyone was supposed to understand and that exists beyond our control. I have spent years of my life shaking an envisioned fist at the sky, cursing a perceived injustice, and crying to well-trained parental ears about the treatment I believed fate was giving me versus what I thought I deserved. I have given my heart and had it severely broken more times than what I would consider to be fair. The heart finds ways to repair itself.

There are some ways in which I view love and my relationship to it to be the most personal of personal experiences and other ways in which I can remove myself from the center and see it as part of a much more complex and socially constructed picture. In speeches I give and presentations

I make, particularly those to kids, I am often asked about whether or not I am married. And this question makes sense because my existence as a woman with a disability can violate so many of the expectations that society has built for people, in general. The rights of passage, like marriage, starting a family, and building a life and identity around that family are expectations for most but guarantees for none. But then there are many more people who assume for me what they have been taught to assume for people with disabilities in general—that they simply do not embody the same wants and desires that other people do. This is so much the case, in fact, that the mere thought of disability and sexuality or romance, taken together, makes people uncomfortable. *We can talk about disability and we can talk about sexuality, but let's not even think about talking about them together.* That's a trend that needs to meet its conclusion, as it is detrimental to everyone. I know it has been detrimental to me.

For many years after my accident, I took it as a given that my paralysis necessarily meant that a long-term relationship and family of my own would never be realities for me. I remember, as a child and even young adult, that beauty, desirability, and the relational outcomes of these characteristics were sacrosanct and reserved for someone else. I felt a sense of inevitability born out of circumstance, a sense of resignation due to intractability. Because of this, I have also felt immeasurable agony, like my heart could not be shattered in a sufficient number of pieces to represent its fragility, and like there was something fundamentally and shamefully wrong with me.

When you live with a physical disability, it is often as if there is a secret about life that no one is telling you or even believes you have a right to know. This is true in the domains of employment, education, and politics, but never truer than in the domain of love.

LOVE AS A HUMAN RIGHT

The divide between disability and sexuality is so much of an instantiated taboo—thankfully receding, but a taboo nonetheless—that the U.N. Convention on the Rights of Persons with Disabilities (CRPD) had to implement a specific article, Article 23, that addressed the need for full participation among people with disabilities when it comes to such things as relationships, love, sexuality, and marriage. Addressing signatory and ratifying nations participating in the U.N. CRPD, statement one of Article 23 states:

1. States Parties shall take effective and appropriate measures to eliminate discrimination against persons with disabilities in all matters relating to marriage, family, parenthood, and relationships, on an equal basis with others, so as to ensure that:
    a. The right of all persons with disabilities who are of marriageable age to marry and to found a family on the basis of free and full consent of the intending spouses is recognized;
    b. The rights of persons with disabilities to decide freely and responsibly on the number and spacing of their children and to have access to age-appropriate information, reproductive, and family planning education are recognized, and the means necessary to enable them to exercise these rights are provided;
    c. Persons with disabilities, including children, retain their fertility on an equal basis with others.[13]

The U.N. CRPD was adopted in December 2006 and began taking signatures in March 2007. Its purpose was to:

> [C]hange attitudes and approaches to persons with disabilities. It takes to a new height the movement from viewing persons with disabilities as "objects" of charity, medical treatment, and social protection toward viewing persons with disabilities as "subjects" with rights, who are capable of claiming those rights and making decisions for their lives based on their free and informed consent as well as being active members of society.[14]

The adoption and ratification of the CRPD meant that, until late 2006 and into 2007, it was still simply taken as given that an individual with a disability could regularly and systematically be denied the right to marry or begin a family. Until late 2006, it was simply taken as given that people with disabilities were not capable enough to bring children into the world and that their forced sterilization was an act of mercy rather than a human rights abuse.

As horrifying as this appears, and it appears to be quite horrifying, there is a history and a reason behind this article of the CRPD. Though love and desire and companionship are critical to human existence, people with disabilities have not always experienced these aspects of humanity in the ways that many others have. In fact, when it comes to sexuality, people with disabilities often experience an unwanted and abusive amount of attention or, on the other extreme, nothing at all, and this dichotomy has relegated many people with disabilities to one or both of the opposing extremes rather than somewhere in the healthy, human in-between. We have needed a U.N. convention to protect these rights. We have needed a

U.N. convention to even begin to talk and think about how fundamental emotions and human experiences present themselves in entirely maladaptive and perverse ways for those whose participation is not expected or whose existence is not valued in the way that it should be.

The staggering and unacceptable prevalence of sexual assault and sexual violence in our society affects people from all demographic and socioeconomic backgrounds. Sexual violence is a power-driven sociological scourge to which no one is immune, although some are more susceptible. Yet, despite the fact that we care not to think about disability and sexuality in the same context, it is people with disabilities who are most likely to be survivors of sexual assault. It is notoriously difficult to collect data among people with disabilities on any issue, as, due to social stigma, many people do not feel comfortable even disclosing the presence of a disability. Nevertheless, a very conservative and most certainly under-estimated assessment is that 83 percent of women with disabilities will be sexually assaulted in their lives. Similarly, women with a disability are far more likely to have undesired sex with an intimate partner, at a rate of 19.7 percent versus 8.2 percent among those without disabilities. Among those who have a developmental disability, a staggeringly small 3 percent of sexual abuse instances will ever be reported.[15]

Research has shown that people with disabilities, particularly intellectual disabilities, are sexually assaulted at a rate seven times higher than people without disabilities.[16] What makes this finding that much more disturbing is that these individuals are more likely to be assaulted by someone they know, in the broad light of day, because they can so easily be manipulated, especially by people they believe they can trust. When considering people with intellectual disability, justice is almost never pursued and even more rarely gotten, as these human beings can have difficulty answering questions, can have difficulty constructing a narrative, and can easily be led astray or become uncertain. Or they believe that their stories will go ignored.

Across disability, there is a frightening epidemic of sexual abuse that has been described as "unrecognized, unprosecuted, and unpunished." The egregious overrepresentation of people with disabilities among sexual assault victims should not be tolerated and, in fact, would not be tolerated if it were seen in essentially any other population. As tragic and as staggering as these circumstances are on face value, there are sociocultural factors that make them that much more complex and grueling. Not all people with disabilities understand their relationship with sexual violence in the same way, and the particularities of these relationships are almost never discussed.

There is an aversion to discussing sexuality and disability—even in these times, even among people who freely discuss sex, and even among people with disabilities themselves. It is easier to turn away than it is to shine a light on the nuances that lie at the intersection of sexuality and disability: how the marginalization of people with disabilities can force them to find comfort from people who do not have their best interests in mind; how people with disabilities can be stereotyped as nonsexual or nondeserving of an intimate relationship and, as a result, can be disrespected as such; and how these factors, taken together, can cause one of two equally destructive outcomes: the involvement in an abusive relationship or the self-defeating notion that sexual assault is the privileged result of those deemed sexually desirable. None of these ought to be tolerated, and they only have been tolerated for as long as they have because we, as a society, have not mastered the language needed to talk about disability and sexuality and love in a meaningful way. Talking about sex and disability in one conversation is as much about sexuality as it ought to be about how power imbalances and social hierarchies can directly affect people's understanding of themselves, as sexual beings and as people of worth.

Disability is not lovable—that was what I assumed, just as many others assume. That assumption was as illogical as it was unfortunate, and it was as culturally constructed as it was needlessly perpetuated. I have thought far too little of myself and possibly too little of those who surround me. Now, years later, I can understand this and can realize how much these beliefs were indoctrinated by a world and society that has never seen disability for what it truly is, for the value and beauty that it truly adds. I can also see how much I wish I had had the resolve and individual strength to combat those beliefs before they developed the impetus to shape my thinking and, thus, my life. But I didn't then. I was too timid as a child, too unsure of myself as a person in a marginalized identity to question the social constructs that were put upon it, and I was too fearful of never being loved to want to call attention to its absence in my life. "Let it go," I would think to myself, "don't waste your time on what isn't realistic."

This is not at all to imply that people with disabilities do not find love or romantic relationships. As a matter of fact, there are many who do, and it is those very relationships that outwardly call the bluff of those who don't but might have. For me, love and romance have been life entitlements that have existed tauntingly just beyond my most extended reach. There is an injustice that I feel about this perception that I placed on my life—years of opportunity and possibility that I denied myself or felt were stolen from me. There have been days when I have stared into the mirror, wondering what it is about myself that people do not see but I know to be true. I have wondered if I were not pretty enough or if I were not smart enough or if I were not funny enough or engaging enough or skinny enough. I thought all of these things until I finally thought, *enough*. I am enough of all of these things. My life is not a quest to get someone else to understand that, it has been a quest to get me to understand that.

MY LIFE IS A LOVE STORY

I am a woman, complete with all of the sexuality, sensuality, sensitivity, and humanity that womanhood embodies. I want to love and to be loved by somebody. My desire to be touched or embraced where and when I want to does not lie fallow at the foot of my wheelchair. I am sexual, maybe even inordinately so. I find beauty and love in many from all backgrounds, without discrimination. I crave touch, especially on my face and lips, where so much of my body's sensitivity is concentrated and therefore heightened that the slightest and most delicate touch, applied appropriately, is potent to the point of being erogenous. I don't see anything shameful about that want—that need. It is as fundamental a part of me as a human as is my need for water. But one of the lessons that is learned through life with disability is that expectations of and judgments about your body disrupt the ways that people understand the rest of who you are. I am a sexual person just as I am a sensual person, but on the hierarchy of needs that pertain to love, those qualities are on bottom rung.

The fact of the matter is that my life story is a love story.

There are many things on which I could conceivably define my life, and many of these are more obvious than others. But at this point in my life, when I have likely lived the majority of it and have seen so many sides of it, I choose to define my life in a way that I want it to be understood. My life is a life of love, love that I give with caution but also without need for reciprocity. My life is a life of love, and it is this love that makes me who I am infinitely more than any other characteristic that can be associated with me.

I love to laugh. I have shed my fair share of tears, but my life is one that is drawn along my ever-deepening laugh lines. My colleague Carlos Vidal described laughter and humor as "*sofrito*," or the very thing that gives life its flavor. I know that this statement is true, and it is true across all circumstances, in all contexts.

When I laugh, the sound of my laughter fades in and fades out, due to the air received from my ventilator, but it is constant in its intensity. It is a unique laugh, more silent than it is boisterous, but its passion is no function of its volume. More often than not, I laugh until I cry, with steady streams of tears trekking down my face. It's the only way I know how to do it. If you have found a way to make me laugh, then you have also found the first step into my heart. I have made it a personal quest to surround myself with people who make me laugh, with the people who can remind me of the brightest isolated moments of life and how they are visible even when it seems all of the chips are down. Laughter is the antidote to pain, the salve that soothes a wounded heart and weary soul. And in that laughter, really, is love.

I love to talk. I love to talk so much that I made a profession out of it. I am not a singer (I would spare anyone of that!), but I am a talker—sometimes fast to pay homage to my New York background, sometimes slow to acknowledge a more regularly paced way of life. I never fully understood how much I liked to talk until I was at risk of not being able to talk anymore, and my talking is one of the most intimate things I engage in.

My family is not known for its verbosity, and by nature, we are not storytellers. But the person you believe yourself to be is not always the person that life and circumstance nudge you to become. I have shared my story far and wide, both out of desire and out of necessity, as the best way I knew how to transform the immensity of my experience into something usable and of value to those outside of the confines of my own head was via voice. But it is not the grandiose speeches or presentations that I give that are of most consequence, it is my conversations, both intimate and in-depth. I can sit and talk for hours, needing nothing more than an open heart ready for conversation. And in those conversations, really, is love.

I love to learn. I am one of the only people I know who has spent some twenty-five years of her life in the classroom but has no desire to find her way out of it. Many of the people who have changed my life more than anyone have been my teachers, at every step of my life, and they have changed my life because they change the way I think and the clarity with which I see the world. Mr. Stow, my sixth-grade teacher, taught me how to diagram sentences and offered my first exposure to *Cosmos*, which drove my love for writing and my love for science, which ultimately conjoined in my love for writing about science. The words I speak are the culmination of all that I have learned.

My growth as a person who uses a wheelchair was not marked on the molding of a doorway. For all intents and purposes, I have remained one height for thirty years. My growth as a person who uses a wheelchair has taken place almost entirely in my head. From within the halls of the world's most recognized academic institutions to the exchanges I have with people from my own local communities who have lived through experiences vastly different from and sometimes more difficult than my own, I have learned how my role in the world is the culmination of not what my body prevents me from doing but of what it does, what it feels, and what it knows, both about itself and about others. And in that knowledge, really, is love.

I love to be inspired to be better. One of the biggest gifts I have been given is the ability to share my life with people. But it is not my sharing my life with others that is, in and of itself, meaningful, it is the many stories I have heard from people who have reciprocated by sharing their lives with me. In each correspondence, I am given an insight or experience that shapes my thinking and gives me another perspective from which to understand how people live their lives and how they get through each day. Each of these provides an opportunity for me to see myself differently and to change as a result.

Inspiration is a tricky word to use among people within the disabled population, and sometimes with good reason. There are some people with disabilities who reject the title of "inspiration" and don't want to be seen as a mechanism by which other people find meaning in their own lives. But I fail to see the logic in this objection. I can think of no better gift or more valuable way to spend our lives than as a clearer lens or more discerning filter for people to see value in theirs. I want to inspire someone else just as much as I want someone else to inspire me—to help me to see parts of myself that I still don't understand and ways I can do more or be more than I ever knew I could. And in that inspiration, really, is love.

I love my friends. There is an unfortunate reticence that I think many of us have in telling the people in our lives how much they mean to us, almost as if that admission is also an admission of some deficiency or weakness that we would not be willing to accept in ourselves were these people not there. I know my many weaknesses. I know the many deficits that my life can harbor, but I also know all the people who balance my weaknesses with strength and fill my deficits with love. I have a tattoo on the top of my right hand—a delicate, pencil-like drawing of an anchor whose rope becomes a string of birds flying toward the sky. This very same image is tattooed onto the left wrist of my dear friend Michael. Michael and I have a friendship that is unique, having found each other when friendship was what we both needed most. Michael was at my doorstep the day I returned home from the hospital and never left my side since, even if "at my side" had to be at a distance. Over the thirty years that Michael and I have been friends, we have watched each other cry, shouldered each other's pain, shared all of the moments that make life worth living, and have never thought twice about it. Michael is my wings, I am his anchor, and we both would have it no other way.

There is no better reflection of who I am than the one cast, collectively, by my friends. When I give speeches, I am often asked who my heroes are, and my answer over all of these years has never wavered: My heroes are my friends, those people who have given my life all of its richness and color, who make me laugh, talk, and think, who inspire me to be a better person and are better than I could ever hope to be. I define my life by the friendships that sit at the heart of it—friends who have lasted my entire life, friends who have entered my life when they were needed most desperately, friends who have seen my life at its hardest and chose to never look away. In those friendships, really, is love.

I love my family. Most people love their family, so this is not especially surprising. But when a family experiences such an overwhelming fracturing of its known way of life and its vision for its future, family—in whatever form that takes—becomes all there is, or at least all that matters. I would sit with my family in the dayroom of Children's Specialized Hospital, and all of the ways in which our lives had been upended would seem right again. My father, my mother, Kysten, and Reed—the four directions on my compass, the four corners of my world.

There is not one single thing that I have achieved or undertaken in my life that I can claim credit for without also giving credit to my family. They are the framework on which every castle I have built or hoped to build stands. They are the light in my smile, the breath behind my words, and the road on which my past and future have been paved. And with the addition of my nephews—Carter, James, Harrison, Oliver, and Theodore—I have come to understand that the words "I love you" from a child change the contours of your heart, even if that child is not your own. My family, the original five of us now more than doubled in size, has been all the evidence I need of one of life's most baffling lessons: that the space within the human heart is finite yet infinite, and that my family both occupies the space for and is the embodiment of love.

I have yearned for love in my life, the kind of love that we visualize as essential to our existence as humans and the kind of love that happens in a specific way at a generalized point in our lives. I have shed countless tears and wasted countless days hoping for something that may or may not ever present itself for me.

But love is not something that can be defined or understood in its absence. Love is in the here and in the now, no less beautiful, identity-forming, or individualizing in any one form as opposed to another. All of the love that I have in my life is what makes me who I am, and I would not change any aspect of it. It is because of the love in my life that I know, by definition, how lovable I am. It is because of all of the beauty in my life that I know beauty can be found in me. It is because of the value I bring to my relationships in the world around me that I know I am, in myself and with no imagined changes, infinitely valuable. I am made better by the world and the world is made better by me, and I love that about myself. I love that I know that, and I love that the world I have built around me knows it too.

7

I HOPE

We will face darkness, there is no question about that,
but the darkness that we perceive does not guarantee or
even imply the absence of light.

TRAGEDY PROVIDES NO WARNING. TRAGEDY is a stealthy and opportunistic opponent that is both indiscriminate in its target and seemingly punitive in its existence. These are near-universal truths about an aspect of the human experience that few of us want to acknowledge or spend too much time thinking about. It is easier for almost all of us to live our lives without the omnipresent concern of what tragedy might befall us and when. To be sure, most of us couldn't get through our daily lives or do all of the things we need to do to remain productive if we were always aware of what might be waiting for us each day. That is healthy; that is foundational to a positive and well-adjusted life.

But there is unfortunately no correlation between our unwillingness to focus on the potential sources of trauma or tragedy and the likelihood of these things, in fact, taking place. We can't force tragedy to keep its distance by either not thinking about it or by thinking about it too much. It presents itself on its own timeline and in the form of its own choosing. And each time, it is devastating. It is unmooring. It is disorienting, and it is seemingly all-encompassing, like our lives have been uprooted and are no longer recognizable as our own. I know all of these things to be true, as I have undergone all of them, but I have also come out on the other side.

My family and I experienced a tragedy, but my life is not tragic. There are some who espouse the hackneyed but from-a-distance-empowering idea that the things that don't kill us make us stronger, but I don't believe that to be necessarily true. A survey of humanity would likely tell us that many people suffer greatly in the challenges they undergo, and that their lives are sometimes severely impacted in ways we don't even fully understand. There are others who say that the events in our lives are meant to be, part of a prescribed or otherwise uncontrollable trajectory that ultimately brings us to where we need to be. I don't necessarily believe things are meant to be, but I do believe we can find meaning in even what seem to be the most meaningless circumstances.

THE FUNDAMENTALS OF HOPE

I am an ardent believer in the power of hope. The looseness and ubiquity with which we use such an important word like "hope" has diluted its significance and has eroded what I believe to be proactive work and tangible steps required to foster it. Each of us can merely hope for things to happen—to get a particular job, to take a particular vacation, to meet a particular person—but that isn't what I mean when I talk about "hope" as a concept. Hope is much more than that. Hope is an action statement, a commitment, and a willingness to not just believe but to take steps to ensure that a different and better outcome can be achieved.

I studied hope as a psychological construct when I was an undergraduate student at Harvard. In order to understand hope as an action-based idea, rather than an amorphous and wishful one, I needed to understand it in the context of what takes place in our brains and in our bodies when we experience trauma. There is nothing fundamentally wrong with saying something like, "I hope it doesn't rain on my wedding day" or stating aloud some other outcome we want to effectuate by turning our attention to it. We all do it, often many times a day. In fact, an argument can be made that we need to do that for our own sense of stability in the world. In these cases, "hope" is a verb essentially synonymous with "wish" or "want." But there is an important thread running through each of these verbs: *hope for, wish that, want to*. Each of these verbs places the locus of action somewhere else, on some external or ethereal force that will somehow intervene to bring the outcome into existence. We outsource the steps between origin and outcome to something else, even mere happenstance, and let the pieces fall where they may. This third-party-interventionist approach to hope is useful in some cases, but that isn't how I choose to interpret it.

The experience of trauma is not only life altering, it is brain altering. When we experience trauma, not only does it feel like everything around us becomes unrecognizable, there are parts of our anatomy, or neuroanatomy, that also become unrecognizable. In order to understand how, it is important to understand a bit of the complexity of the brain. There is a great deal about the brain that we—or neuroscientists—have yet to uncover. The human brain is a frontier of scientific exploration that is in many ways uncharted. But there are also many neurological understandings that provide some elemental insight into how humans respond to traumatic events.

Many neuroscientists and experts on the psychology of decision-making have proposed that the human brain operates in accordance with two different mental processes: one that produces instinctive or automatic responses to stimuli around us, and one that produces more deliberate and controlled responses.[17] The automatic or instinctive responses our brains produce are fast, often spontaneous, and largely sensory in nature. As behavioral economist Daniel Kahneman theorized, we rely on our automatic thinking in the same way that we rely on other evolutionary and reflexive responses—to think faster than our deliberate thinking allows us to think; to be the mechanism of action to flee if necessary when the slowness of processed thinking encompasses more time than we, in fact, have.[18] The oft-cited examples of this type of thinking are plentiful: our pulling a hand away from a hot stove before our brain has understood the heat; our recoiling at loud noises or slithering objects; our spitting out of food that is spoiled. We do these things before we even have the chance to think about them.

As helpful and as necessary as automatic thinking is to our very survival, it cannot and should not account for all the types of thoughts that humans require to live their lives fully. The other system of thinking, the more deliberate and reasoned kind, is necessary for the mental processes that need to be slower, more purposeful, more intentional. Our conversations throughout the course of the day demand this type of reasoned thought. The decisions we make to live effectively within society—follow our moral principles, abide by laws and rules, teach our children, complete our work—all of these activities require prudence, intentionality, and more than the reflexivity that our autonomic and automatic thinking can provide.

But emotions and concepts like hope and resilience, the very emotions and concepts that walk beside us as we travel from the origins of trauma to some more peaceful state, exist between these two systems of decision-making, these two seemingly but not necessarily juxtaposing neurological circuits.

In the same context in which I studied hope, I also studied resilience. I have come to understand resilience to be a characteristic or a state of being. Resilience is that quality within us that allows us to adapt to adversity successfully, to reinterpret as opportunities what we initially thought were limitations. Hope is the action we take to become resilient, to develop resilience. Understanding how these ideas fit together is both innately simplistic and, at the same time, one of humanity's most difficult lessons.

Adversity and challenge are fundamental to the human experience. They are as true to each of our lives as is our need for breath and water. And yet, like so many other sources of stress that we encounter, our innate or reflexive response to trauma, challenge, adversity, and difficulty is to remove ourselves from it as quickly as we can. Given the choice, there is almost no one who would remain in a situation of trauma or difficulty. We see it, we feel it, and we want out of it as immediately as possible. When I awoke from a coma only thirty-six hours after my accident, and at so many points in time since then, I wanted to run away—I wanted to create as much distance as I possibly could between myself and the circumstances in which I found myself. I wanted to be rid of all of the things that frightened me, all of the sources of stress, confusion, uneasiness, unfamiliarity. I wanted my life to resemble everything that was previously familiar, everything that gave me a sense of security and wholeness.

But I couldn't. In fact, as our world and as our lives have become more complex, there are many terrifying and unfamiliar circumstances in which we find ourselves that we cannot simply save ourselves from by running away. The current construction of our societies and communities makes us far less likely to encounter a threat that is appropriate for our evolved sense of automatic thinking—like a rattlesnake—and far more likely to encounter a threat that forces us to think, to figure things out. That is where hope is found. That is where resilience is built.

Hope is the whisper that keeps us moving forward when we have every desire to retreat. Hope is the foundation that assures us that we can when the core of our being tells us that we couldn't possibly. Hope is the bridge that connects the challenges we encounter to our ability to process them, sort them out, and then take them on purposefully.

When you live with a disability like quadriplegia, there essentially is not a single day that goes by when you are not confronted with something unfamiliar, challenging, adversarial, or terrifying. It is a rare day that goes entirely as planned or without some—oftentimes many—obstacles of varying severity that complicate how life is lived. It is the wheelchair that chooses, without warning, to fail to operate when you are scheduled to be at a meeting. It is the restaurant that is surprisingly inaccessible or underequipped for catering to the needs of a person with a disability. It is the unfamiliar pain or sore that was not there on Tuesday but sends you to the doctor on Wednesday. It is the trips you had planned but realize you cannot take. It is the love you may hope for but have yet to find. It is the will to move your body that is not met with a response.

These are the daily obstacles that affect the lives of people with disabilities like mine that, though extreme, complicate my life in the very same ways that other peoples' lives are complicated by obstacles. They cause frustration. They make me want to pound my fists on the table. They make me want to scream the details of the injustices to anyone who will listen. They make me want to run away from what is and hide in something better. But all of these intrinsic responses are futile. They do nothing. Change nothing. Save me from nothing other than the opportunity to see the world differently.

Hope is the framework that we can build on to empower ourselves enough to persevere when challenge seems to be at its most unrelenting. While there is not one single day in which I do not rely on hope as the cornerstone of the way I live my life, there are some days and some times when I have to rely on it that much more completely than others.

HOPE AS A PROCESS

Hope is not an outcome; it is the path we take to reach a particular outcome. Hope is a word and concept that is used very loosely in the fields of disability and rehabilitation, so much so, in fact, that its significance and relevance to our lives has become eroded. However, when you undergo a life-altering injury or accident that tests all of your strength, sometimes hope is all you have, and all you can grasp on to. But, rather than looking at hope as an ethereal or mystical idea, I have come to see it as something much more tangible and action-oriented. In his book *The Future of American Progressivism*,[19] Harvard professor Roberto Unger made a valuable and insightful claim: that hope is the consequence of action, not the cause. Based on the experiences I have undergone, times in which my sense of personal agency and motivation were tested, I can see the truth in this idea. I have seen the very creation of hope through refusing to succumb to challenges and, instead, finding ways around them.

The concept of hope has been such an important part of my life that, when I was an undergraduate student, I decided to do my senior honors thesis on hope and how it correlates with resilience. I took a decidedly multidisciplinary approach to the issue—looking at hope from biological, psychological, and psychosocial perspectives. Many of my fellow cognitive neuroscience majors were headed to medical school and, when learning of my thesis topic, would look at me with a good amount of uncertainty, as if hope and resilience had no place in the fields of neuroscience or medicine. But I had seen all too clearly how these two structures were perhaps among the most important aspects of my recovery years before.

So, from the vantage point of both a patient and a person, what do I know about hope? Hope, by its very nature, I believe, is a product of challenge. Or, better said, it's a product of believing that challenge can be overcome. There is a delicate characteristic about hope: It's both something that needs to be developed on one's own, but can only be sustained with the help of those around us. It is something that grows out of challenge, but it is also threatened by challenge. Hope has become nearly synonymous with optimism, yet the two concepts can really be understood as entirely different, if not opposite: optimism being a predisposition or attitude, and hope being an action-oriented, tested aspect of character. At the same time, hope, for all of us, is critical to our lives.

But what does that mean? What does it mean to "have hope" or to "be hopeful," whether in life in general or particularly in the face of a life-changing experience? Well, that question can partially be answered by understanding what it means to *not* have hope. In the face of any kind of life-altering condition or event, its magnitude can immediately become overwhelming, if not all-consuming. For me, the parts of life that seemed understandable, predictable, reliable, and secure became elusive and foreign. Every aspect of my life, no matter how personal, was no longer simply my own—everything from eating to bathing to interacting with friends. Accompanying life-altering events, there is the sense that one's life is no longer within one's own control, or that the life you are living is neither the one you wanted nor ever expected. There are feelings of victimization, and it becomes difficult to imagine how the rest of the world is going on around you without any problem.

This is the case for all of us, irrespective of the nature of the challenge we might be experiencing. Hopelessness leaves us overwhelmed by the circumstances around us. Hopelessness leaves us unfocused and disoriented, as if we are mired in stagnation or ineptitude, like our feet are just too heavy to put one in front of the other. And hopelessness makes us feel alone, like no one could possibly understand the enormity of what we are experiencing or the depth of the pain we are undergoing. But each one of these feelings can be overcome, and that is the very purpose of hope.

I want to be absolutely clear about this: I am, in no way, immune to or fully distanced from the grasp of hopelessness. Hopelessness is a recurring visitor, an emotional foe that never relents and is always ready to prey upon moments of vulnerability. Our ability to combat the perils of hopelessness is, actually, highly influenced by the circumstances at the time and the supports we have available to us when they arise. It is also influenced by our physical will to fight. Despite my understanding of hope and what I believe it to entail, I have been stricken with hopelessness quite often, probably with increasing frequency as I have gotten older.

When I first became paralyzed, I had much of my life ahead of me. Of course, there were no guarantees that I would live each day to see this life, but, as much as it was for anyone else, the manifestations of my potential were yet to come. I envisioned myself standing up and dancing across the room. I envisioned myself falling madly in love, finding someone who would want to build his life alongside of and intertwined with my own. I envisioned being at the center of a troop of kids, each of whom would race the others to wrap herself around my legs. I envisioned washing windows, planting flowers, and purchasing, with feigned resistance, a minivan to shuttle precious cargo here and there. These were not the goals

I had for my life but were the behind-the-scenes expectations and rites of passage I assumed for it. As the years have gone by, and as the time for life's milestones have receded farther into the distance, those losses have made more generalized pain that much more acute. And I have dealt with these instances to varying degrees of success and with wavering amounts of fortitude.

But I don't believe that we should punish ourselves when our feelings of hope erode or when everything begins to feel like too much. We all experience moments like these, and they are important parts of being a human, complete with vulnerability, frustration, and an ability to evaluate certain points in our lives against other points in our lives, as some times simply seem smoother than others. But the times when life is difficult are our times of greatest opportunity. This is not at all to minimize the weight of the burdens we carry or the pain we feel, and it is by no means a simplification of all the insidious ways that hopelessness can infiltrate our thoughts, because these are real and they are impactful. But they are also conquerable. The times of vulnerability are our personal inflection points. They are the temporal locations in our lives when they take a new direction, an unanticipated and uncharted direction, but not necessarily a wrong direction.

←——————→

One question I am often asked is if I ever think about what my life "would have been like" had I not been in the accident I was in and left paralyzed. I understand the motivation behind this question as well as the thinking behind it, as if the life I was leading prior to my accident was the real or natural one that had its own evolution and destination and that that previous version of life and ultimate outcome of it would have been the right one. And it would be disingenuous of me to say that I do not ever fall victim to this mental enticement. I ask myself the what-if questions and dream of the if-only scenarios—*What if I hadn't decided to walk home from school that day? If only I waited five more seconds to cross the street, what would things look like now?*—then follow the path of idealized circumstance after idealized circumstance that results in an idealized outcome of what my life could have been. I could have been a dancer on Broadway. I could have been a doctor practicing in a rural community in need. I could have been a photojournalist capturing important ideas from around the world. But the operative word in each of these sentences is "could," not "would." The expectations and visions we have for our lives are purely hypothetical, no more based in fact and no more "right" than any other configuration of what does or does not happen. There is no "should have been," there only is "is," and the sooner we understand that, the sooner we can make *is* as rich and meaningful as it can be.

These realizations do not come easily nor without a great deal of introspection. Especially when there is immeasurable loss involved, it is almost incomprehensible how that loss does not equate to "worse off" or some other inferior status. But the evaluation of the relative merits and worthiness of our lives—the very activity that causes us to long for some other existence—is the functional opposite of hope. Longing for something else that doesn't exist or cannot be isn't "hoping," it's merely wishing. Hoping is the opposite.

Hope is not the desire for some other existence or reality. Hope is the readiness to accept a particular reality as it is and find the drive and vision to maximize that reality. In negotiation terms, this is called "growing the pie." Two parties might come into a negotiation wanting a certain outcome that can't be achieved given the resources that the other party has at its disposal. We grow the pie by looking at other possibilities or constructions of outcomes that we may not have originally envisioned. In leadership terms, this is called "adaptation" or "adaptive work." When an organization or group finds itself in a state of overall disequilibrium or an environment to which it is unaccustomed, adaptation and adaptive work drive people to persevere through these times of organizational difficulty by holding on to the behaviors or structures that are still effective and discovering and adapting new behaviors that accommodate new realities. All of these ideas are linked. All of these ideas—hope, growing the pie, adaptive work—force us to understand the circumstances we face and then change how we operate to function most effectively within them.

This is not easy. This is not merely a call for bright-side-gazing or "well, at least it's not . . ." to be completed with some other scenario that is ostensibly "worse" than the one currently being experienced. Those kinds of recommendations or attempted pieces of advice are relatively useless because they deny or make meaningless the severity or impact of the difficulty one might be facing. That's not what hope is. Hope is not the willful ignoring of pain, hardship, obstacles, or difficulty. Far from it. Hope is the full acknowledgment of the severity of the situation, complete with the pain it causes or limitations it presents, and finding a way to seek purpose and drive despite them. In other words, hope is not a strategy of optimism, it is fully recognizing the pain we feel and finding a way ahead, nevertheless.

In order to do this, we can appreciate the difficulty we face while not affording it any more power over our lives than it absolutely needs. Trauma and difficulty can seem all-encompassing. When we are facing an extreme bout of adversity or a traumatic experience, it is as if this adversity or trauma is taking hold in every aspect of our lives. Trauma and adversity are veritable contagions that infiltrate all aspects of our thoughts and feelings of capability. But there is no characteristic about trauma or adversity that makes this necessarily so; it is often our understanding and interpretation of the adversity we face that give it its magnitude and scope. And this is to be expected, as disaggregating parts of our lives from the uncertainty we feel is notoriously difficult. After my accident, it seemed as though every aspect of my life was turned upside down and nothing was familiar. Lying in my bed in the rehabilitation hospital, I would spend almost every night staring into the ceiling tiles, trying to find some meaning or purpose to all I had lost. I would ask myself a litany of introspective questions—how will I live my life if I can't live it the way I know how to live? What will give my life meaning if I can't do all the things that gave it meaning before? Who am I if I can't be who I was?

THE PILLARS OF HOPE

Each of our lives is inherently complex, with different facets that make them as rich and kaleidoscopic as they are. While we mostly shift from one facet of our lives to another relatively seamlessly, there is a fascinating characteristic about adversity and challenge: When we experience it in one aspect of our lives, we almost reflexively begin to associate it with all aspects of our lives. The sense of trauma that can often accompany deep adversity and challenge becomes insidious, making us feel far more disempowered than we need to. By virtue of the barriers that can impede one aspect of our lives, we begin to put up barriers in other, sometimes wholly unrelated, aspects of our lives. This is unnecessary and it robs us of opportunities to explore parts of ourselves that we had not before had the time or inclination to truly appreciate.

This is where the first pillar of hope stands—the first of three. Although challenge and adversity are universal, so, too, is the ability to relegate them to the smallest and least impactful role they can play in our lives. We can compartmentalize the circumstances we face. Circumscribe them. Sequester them. Stop the contagion before it spreads. This is to understand the challenges in our lives without understanding our lives in terms of challenge. Pain and adversity are part of who we are, but they are not all of who we are.

On September 4, 1990, I became paralyzed. On September 4, 1991, I returned to junior high school to move forward with my life. There were many parts of my identity and existence that were gone, and I felt that pain intensely. But it did not necessarily follow that my ability to think, learn, participate in my community, or contribute to the world was also gone. That was not a realization that grew easily or even naturally. That was the indoctrination I gave myself after growing tired of simply counting the ceiling tiles from my hospital bed, trying to find order in the dots. I could continue to focus on my losses, or I could reduce the prominence of those losses by isolating the parts of my life that were unaffected by them.

The day I returned to my junior high school to be with my classmates was terrifying. I had been away from my community and friends for a full year, and many of the people I was closest to had not seen me or inter-acted with me since my accident. While a few of my friends had been able to visit me while I was in the hospital—friends who were closest to me and who were able to take the trip all the way from Long Island to New Jersey—most simply couldn't because of the distance or lack of opportu-nity. I was terrified to see them or, better said, terrified for them to see me. I was afraid that my friends, the very people who were also my avenue to normality, would feel one of two things: pity or discomfort.

Taking this first step, however uncomfortable it may have been for me at the time, was critical to the way I would continue to understand and live my life. Nearly every aspect of my identity and sense of physical pres-ence had changed, and learning to live with these changes would require continual amounts of fortitude. But it was possible to appreciate those losses and changes while directing my thoughts, time, energy, and vision of a future in other ways. I was terrified. I was frustrated. I was unsure of myself. But at the same time, I was motivated. I was adapting. And I was taking ownership over circumstances that I was not going to let take ownership over me.

This is what I believe to be is the second pillar of hope, orienting or reorienting our focus from what we have lost or what we regret to those things we still have and can enjoy. At twelve years old, that was perhaps the most salient and surely most impactful point in my life: when I had to learn not only to relegate the limitations I was facing to the least significant role they could play but also to shift my thinking and focus to some other collection of parts of my identity. I could focus on my losses or I could focus on that which remained. I could long for a life that I no longer had or I could enrich the new life I had. Those were my options, and the former would change nothing while the latter could change everything.

I don't mean for this to sound simple, like it was merely a matter of choosing between two paths like they were menu options. It wasn't easy for me, just as it isn't easy for anyone, and there were many points—thousands, likely, over the years—when I fell victim to the lure of a life that no longer existed. It is impossible not to. As a matter of fact, there is no small number of times when I have spent days or even weeks at a time wallowing in the sadness of all the things I cannot do. While there is no shame to be found in that, there is also no benefit to be gained from it either. There is not one single time when I have looked at my life in terms of loss and then felt better because of it. There has not been one single time when grieving over that which does not exist or the pain I have undergone has brought me closer to the life I want to live. And there has not been one single time when allowing myself to be subsumed by frustration has made things any easier for either myself or anyone around me. And although I know that now about my life, I also know that an awareness of all these facts will not, and maybe even cannot, stop feelings of loss, grief, or frustration from rearing their heads. But I know that I can prevent them from taking over.

I could not have come to this realization on my own, and that might be the most insidious aspect of hopelessness: that it ruthlessly makes people feel alone and deeply isolated. Feelings of hopelessness often take the form of implicit barriers created between the pain we experience and those who love us enough to reduce the extremity of that pain. It would be nice to believe that each of us had the capacity within ourselves to forge ahead in the face of the pain or adversity that we feel, that we all could be willfully self-reliant and find the skills within ourselves to combat all that fate might send our way. Or maybe it wouldn't be very nice at all. Whether or not it is justified to feel isolated in our instances of hopelessness, hopelessness is a shape-shifter and deceiver that makes us feel that way. Hopelessness tempts us into thinking that we are alone and there is no one who can understand the magnitude of the pain we feel. This is where the final component of hope, as I understand it, comes into play.

PERSONAL EMPOWERMENT–THE "-PE" OF HOPE

Hope is self-reinforcing. It builds upon successes in the past and engenders an individualized worldview that becomes part of one's identity. Success after success breeds a behavior pattern and expectation that is predicated on success, and a mindfulness toward possibility begins to overtake one of impossibility. But "personal" empowerment is not necessarily synonymous with empowerment that is "individualized" or "entirely self-actualized." Instead, it is the product of the skills and fortitude we find within us, necessarily bolstered by the people who matter around us. That is essential, and that is a fact. Just as there has been no single time when dwelling on my losses has brought about comfort or solace, there has also been no single time when the shift in my thinking from the pain of loss to the power of possibility was not driven by the love and support of the people around me.

In 2018 I turned forty. Forty is a difficult birthday for many of us, but I think not for the reasons we initially believe. Some view forty as the point at which youth becomes non-youth—that forty is the moment when it is harder to convince oneself that one's life is still in the development phase. But forty is, in actuality, an accomplishment and by no means a guarantee. Forty, though, does ask us to be introspective, to evaluate our lives until that point. Perhaps that's what we fear, an evaluation of our lives that tells us that we did not do all that we could have or wanted to.

I didn't fear turning forty in the way that many people do. In fact, my fortieth birthday was one of the best days of my life. I surrounded myself with all of my closest friends and family for a black-tie masquerade ball, in outdoor tents under the starry October sky. But I was sick. I would soon find out that I was deathly sick, battling not one but four fatal infections and a cavernous pressure sore that was spreading uncontrollably. I knew what the road ahead of me was going to look like—intravenous antibiotics to fight osteomyelitis (infection of the bone), additional powerful and sometimes experimental antibiotics to treat other infections within the wound, surgery to help heal the wound, probable secondary infections or superinfections from antibiotic overexposure, and an indeterminate recuperation time that would likely keep me homebound, if not bedridden, for well over a year.

As my birthday approached, I toyed with the idea of canceling any festivities or celebration. I was inordinately sick and feeling far from festive or celebratory. But given the battles that I knew were ahead of me, I also knew that I needed to have my biggest reserves of strength, sources of support, and generators of hope by my side. In a night that included dinner, dancing, speeches, and more love than I had felt in a very long time, this is what I said to all the guests:

> *Good evening, everyone. Well, if you know anything about me—and I suppose your presence here tonight is evidence that you do—you know that I love to talk, especially when it involves a microphone. So I'm going to use this opportunity to manipulate your dinner hour and your status as captives here to do what I am probably best at and certainly what I enjoy the most—to talk about myself, but not just myself, because any complete and honest thoughts about me would necessarily include all of you. I have said this many times, to many people, but unfortunately not often enough to the people to whom it applies—I am who I am and my life is as beautiful as it is because of all of you.*
>
> *So, just so everyone can get a fuller understanding of who is here: There are my friends from my childhood, who made growing up in Stony Brook the very best place to grow up and gave me a childhood I wouldn't trade if given a choice of ten million others: Suzie, Eileen, Mary, Elizabeth, John Paul, Jackie, John.*
>
> *There are friends who came into my life when friends were what I desperately needed to learn to re-understand myself: Debbie, Zach, Deb and Ernie, Chris and Rich, Matt, and, of course, Michael, who, as you can tell, is always at my side.*
>
> *There are my friends from college, who are the very*

heart and soul of what was, by far, the most transformative time in my life, when I learned to become myself, when I learned that I could understand my life in terms of possibility, resilience, and hope: Cara, Kawuan, John, Gattnar, Abraham.

There are friends from graduate school, where I learned that the world is a flawed but no less beautiful place and that it is up to us to change it for the better, and that we can: Alison, Jeff, Steve.

There are friends from work, at Stony Brook, who have helped me to grow and from whom I have learned, and with whom I have been fortunate to embark on meaningful ways to change people's lives: Ghenet, Matthew, Saeedah, Josué.

And there are friends who have entered my life over the years in the most unexpected ways, who have enriched my life through ways as diverse as from music to science and have allowed me to share my life with theirs: Jake, Todd, Robbye and Anne-Marie, Francine, Justin, Matt, Michael.

There is my extended family, my aunts, uncles, cousins, who have helped shoulder enormous heartache and have supported me through moments of exhilaration: Margaret, Lee, Amy, Trudy, Emmy, Joe, Michelle, Chris and Stacey, Tracy and Frank, Kelly and Vinny, Patrick, Justin, Nick.

And there is my family—Mom, Dad, Kysten, Reed, Dave, Ellen (and Carter, Jamie, and Harrison, whose heads are too small for masks)—the people who I could never, nor ever want to, do without. The people to whom I owe every single day of my life, the people who mean every-thing to me and have never asked anything in return. You all exemplify the very best parts of my life because you are the very best parts of my life.

As some of you know, and some to a greater extent than others, this year has been a difficult one for me, with some health issues that have, at times, been challenging. But challenge is no stranger to me, and what I have learned from it over the years is that it is a meager opponent to love. These are the times when you need to fight, and it's so much easier to fight when you have filled your life with people who make it that much more worth fighting for. You are the story of my life. You are the true Brooke Ellison Story. And today, October 20, is my fortieth birthday—a milestone that, for many, is approached with dread or at least reluctance. But I love my birthday—even my forti-eth birthday—because every passing year is a testament to the fortitude and resilience and commitment it took to get there. A testament to all of you, actually. So, of all the ways that I could have chosen to celebrate my fortieth birthday, none would have been complete without you here.

If you know anything else about me, you also know that I love science and, in many ways, dedicate my life to it. Science is rational, science explains the seemingly inex-plicable, science can measure the seemingly immeasurable. But one thing that science has not been able to rationalize, explain, or measure is love. Thank you all, for teaching me what science cannot—that the finite space in my heart can hold an infinite amount of love.

I used this opportunity to individually recognize many of the people closest to me who served as my sources of strength and support over the years, knowing that I would need this very same strength and support moving ahead. We are empowered by the presence of the people around us. Without a doubt, a will to carry on despite hardships and difficulty must be found within oneself, but our ability to ultimately survive and then thrive is just as undoubtedly built upon the structures that are put into place by those we love and who love us. Accepting this reality is much more difficult than it might initially appear, though. We are taught from a perhaps unreasonably young age the centrality of such virtues as ingenuity, individual responsibility, and self-reliance, which, while all isolated components of an overall ability to adjust to changing dynamics in which we find ourselves, are qualities that in and of themselves could not ever be enough to carry us through the points when our own sense of self is wavering. In other words, self-reliance and individuality are the qualities by which we become stronger within ourselves and crystallize a representation of the person we would like to become, but there are moments—many more than any of us might care to believe—when that understanding of ourselves or our general sense of self is far less resolute.

We need the care and comfort of people in our lives to put us back together when we are at risk of crumbling. They are our buttresses, our reinforcements, when we, on an individual basis, have difficulty fighting on our own.

HOPE IN ACTION

It was November 2006, and I had just completed my campaign for New York State Senate. I had put my heart and soul into my campaign, spending weeks developing policy ideas and positions on issues I cared deeply about, months knocking on doors and meeting voters across New York State's second senate district every day, hours sharing with them my thoughts about Long Island's future and hearing theirs, days attending community functions and organization meetings, meeting with unions, media, religious leaders, organizers. It was a privilege. I saw it as a means to reconnect government with the people it is designed to serve. I saw my involvement in it as a chance to restore a faith in our politics, that it is and ought to be a force for making people's lives better, and that at the point at which we had lost the primacy of that vision, we had gone astray.

I know that belief to be a noble one—one that should be at the heart of any political candidate's understanding of the political landscape. The ideas and negative connotations that we ascribe to politics and politicians are the products of a failure to appreciate that politics is not a vehicle for self-aggrandizement or individual maximization, it is a vehicle for societal growth and the ways we bring about the best in everyone. When the electoral results of the campaign came in and I lost, I felt like I was being rejected by the very people I was hoping to serve. That feeling was devastating. It was violating. It was a rejection of everything I believed to be true about the world.

For several weeks after the election, I was directionless and I was rudderless, without a sense of where I was heading and without the will to get there. Some of the things that I thought made sense in my life were no longer making any sense at all, and everything that was familiar was foreign again. I didn't want to see people. I didn't want to leave my house and bump into somebody who had worked on my campaign or who wanted to give me a piece of political advice. I wanted to be alone, to think my own thoughts, and to find my own way. But after three weeks of this, I was no closer to *finding my own way* than I was the day after the election. My parents were getting worried about me. I was even getting worried about me.

In 2006 Reed was living in Boston, contemplating a move back to New York. After graduating from Tufts in 2002, he stayed in the Boston area to get his MBA and MS in accounting. He started a job in a public accounting firm that took him all over the globe, and we didn't get to see each other nearly often enough. Reed was going to give it his best shot to be home for Thanksgiving. But it would be a very fast turnaround time, given his work schedule, and it might not even make sense at all, given the snowy weather expected immediately before the holiday.

It was the weekend before Thanksgiving, and my mother and I were going over our tradition of getting out the family recipes, beginning some of the baking, and cozying up for the holiday season. I wanted my heart to be in it, but it wasn't nearly as much as it should have been. We were looking over the pumpkin bread recipe when the front door opened. My brother shouted, "I'm home!" as he dragged in a bag of laundry. It didn't take very long for me to put the unassembled puzzle pieces together. My brother had come home, not just for the holiday but well in advance of it, to be with me and to help me through a deeply emotional time. It was not so much that the outcome of the election had not gone in my favor—that was incidental and a clear possibility before I even began my campaign. It was much more the fact that I felt a bit lost, like I needed to regain a sense of my roots and my identity. Having Reed at my side was the perfect antidote to the directionlessness I was feeling.

Over the course of the following few days, my brother and I spent hour after hour sitting in my bedroom—television on in the background—talking about our lives. We talked about our childhood together and how inseparable we were as children. We talked about how we would ride our bicycles through the trees in our backyard pretending that they were hiking trails and that we were headed off on fantastical adventures. We talked about how we would play "molten lava" each night, jumping from the couch to the lounge chair to scattered pillows on the floor to steer clear of the imagined threat that the carpet-turned-volcano-contents posed to our little feet. And we talked about times of sorrow in our lives that could only be understood as less-than-sorrowful by talking about them together: the months we spent apart as a family when I was in the hospital and how that happened at such an impressionable age for all of us, but also how we found joy and comfort in that experience that so few ever have. Then we talked about our lives as they were at the time. We talked about relationships in each of our lives that were going either as we had or had not hoped. We talked about life on Long Island versus life in Boston and how both of those locations accounted for valuable real estate in our hearts. And then we talked about our lives going forward and what we might expect out of them. Reed told me that he was planning to move back to New York and spend some time in New York City to find what opportunities might exist there. We talked about our hopes of finding the right person to spend our lives with and the families we might have. And we talked about the topic that no child wants to talk about—what their lives might be like without their parents around.

Before we realized it, it was Sunday of Thanksgiving weekend, and I had spent the previous week remembering how much I had to be thankful for. Hope was restored for me, brought about by the strength of someone I loved dearly who could help me find myself again, who could help me restore my focus to the parts of myself that were real and immutable, and then maximize them to the greatest extent possible. And this is what I know hope to be in simplest terms. We will face darkness, there is no question about that, but the darkness that we perceive does not guarantee or even imply the absence of light. We can and do find those isolated and sometimes dim points of light, and we can go after them. Cling to them. Find solace in them. And find the people who bring us closer to them.

8

←———→

LEADERSHIP

The "finding of our voice" is not the finding of something that has been lost, it is the recapturing of our ideas.

AS A GIFT TO MYSELF for my thirtieth birthday, I got a small tattoo. In the years that I have had it, it has begun to fade a bit, but the sentiment beneath the delicate cursive lettering that reads "*Imagine*" has remained resolute and unwavering. I got this particular tattoo as an homage to the eponymous song, but it also serves as a reminder. An imperative state-ment, of sorts, to think bigger, to think with more clarity of purpose, and to think with more imagination than I might. This is a lesson that I have honed, but it is a skill I have by no means perfected, as it takes constant training. Daily reminders. Chronic learning, to become intrinsically aware that the changes in our lives demand changes within ourselves. I've come to understand that living with a disability often demands multiplicative and multifaceted manifestations of creativity and imagination in ways that can test the boundaries of human creativity and the human imagination. This was a realization that was, by no means, intuitive or reflexive or even quick in its presentation. Instead, the realization of my ability to view not only challenges but also possibilities from multiple vantage points took time. It took patience. And it took a belief in myself.

In the years after I graduated from Harvard in 2000, I faced a point of significant doubt and struggle. I had just completed four of the most stimulating and engaged years of my life, an experience that typically puts people in positions of enormous privilege to accept jobs or internships or opportunities of other kinds that simply are not afforded to many. Yet, after graduating from Harvard, I felt that many of these same doors were not opened for me in the same way. In fact, I felt as though many of the doors had at least three steps up to them. My years at Harvard, especially my senior year as I got close to graduation, were a flurry of activity taking place amidst the bustling Harvard Square. Returning home to Long Island struck a different pace—one that was dictated by self-discipline and self-direction. Living with a disability is a life led unconventionally, as conventions are not always feasible or practical, given the physical demands that people can face. As a result of this disparity in opportunity, people with disabilities become self-starters—authors, journalists, photographers, public speakers, bloggers, web designers, consultants—the kinds of occupations that allow for flexibility and diversity in lifestyle.

Following my graduation, though, I was presented with the opportunity to set out on a course that doesn't emerge often or for many. I had come to learn that, when opportunities present themselves, you do your best to try to seize them. I spent two years writing and working as a public speaker. This work took me to places I had thought I would likely not see—the halls of junior high schools and high schools, campgrounds used as retreats for children grappling with the complexities of mental illness, churches, and civic groups meeting sites. Over the course of several years, I spoke in front of audiences of all kinds, sharing my life and story in ways I had never done before. I spoke personally, about difficult parts of my life that I had often been reluctant to share. I spoke in a way that I thought would bring me closer to and allow me to connect with people who had never undergone anything even resembling my experiences but found it important to connect with me, like we were united in our struggle, joined by something existing beyond daily life.

There is both an intimacy and a self-awareness that comes out of sharing parts of your life with people who would otherwise be strangers. I didn't know this fact before I started working as a public speaker, but I know it now, as it has provided me with the opportunity to become a stronger and more reflective version of myself. Whenever I give speeches, I share parts of my life experiences—my life before my accident, how the impact of my accident forced me to reevaluate how I would live my life moving forward, and the events that had transpired since that time and that realization. The story takes an arc of its own—one built on an existence sent into an unexpected and uncertain trajectory, only to find a steady course in a different orbit. I was in one place and advancing in one direction, and although I did not ever ask for it, I was sent wildly off course. It is that shifting of direction that is so disorienting. It is that belief that the original course was the right course and the new one is some inferior version of the predicted path that is so unsettling. But we find a home even in unfamiliarity. Every road has a forward direction.

My experiences are, in many ways, an amplified version of the kinds of adjustments we all need to make when we have undergone an unexpected and, oftentimes, undesired change in our lives. We are forced to rethink what we do and to rethink our relationship with the world. We are forced to do things differently and sometimes forced to do them better. The universality of this problem connects my life to the lives of the people to whom I speak.

I conclude essentially every speech I give with an opportunity for questions and answers, a period of time in which I can speak more candidly and extemporaneously, and a time in which people often share parts of their lives with me. This is my favorite part of any speech-giving session I have done. There is a risk factor and vulnerability that must be assumed when you say to an audience, "You can ask me anything, don't be shy." But it's also hugely liberating. I head into every speech I give with the presumption that I have explored all sides of myself, that I have viewed the prism from all angles. Yet unfailingly, in the questions that are asked of me and stories that I sometimes share without having expected to share them, I learn something surprising—both about myself and about humanity. Working as a public speaker allowed me to claim ownership over my story and how I wanted to tell it. There is a power in finding your voice and claiming it. I was not aware of this phenomenon when I originally began public speaking but have since come to understand it and have seen how this is true. It is often unclear what people mean when they say, "I found my voice," like our "voices," and therefore our thoughts, can somehow elude us. But that perspective looks at the issue from the wrong direction. When we undergo some kind of difficulty or traumatic experience, it is almost assuredly disempowering. It is like the vocabulary—and, therefore, the very reality—that we use to make sense of our lives has evaporated. Like it no longer exists. Finding our voice is the antithesis of that systematized disempowerment.

When we undergo an acute trauma or stressful event, it is not just the weight of the emotions that make us feel unmoored and directionless. There are actual changes that take place in our brains when we are under prolonged stress or are experiencing trauma. These cognitive changes affect processes that take place in our prefrontal cortex, which is a part of the brain that manages our higher cognitive functioning, like working memory. A considerably prolonged stressor or the manifestations of an ongoing trauma can sometimes lead to long-term damage to the neurons in the prefrontal areas of our brains.[20]

For decades now, neuroscientists have been studying the structural changes that take place in the brain in response to fear and trauma. When we talk about our brains' responses to trauma, we talk about the quick and autonomic reactions based in the fight-or-flight response initiated by our brains' amygdalae. The connection of the amygdala to other brain structures triggers a hormone response in our pituitary and adrenal glands, which initiates the increased production of cortisol, our primary stress hormone. This response is necessary and is the product of millennia of evolution and was well-suited for the types of fears or dangers that humans experienced in centuries past. And when the stressor was removed, usually the response concluded also.

But those immediate and addressable threats are not the types of stressors or traumatic experiences that we, as complex human beings living in a complex world, experience today. The prolonged and intense nature of our mental and emotional stress can sometimes initiate all sorts of changes in our brain cells. But this neurological change is not prescriptive, and there are ways to change it, just as there have always been ways to unlearn the fear-based responses we have. Time and time again, it has been demonstrated that compassionate and strong social relationships have a positive effect on our overall mental and physical health. The very fact of having social connections and a support system has consistently been associated with lower risk of psychopathology and lower risk of negative consequences brought about by physical and emotional stressors. But in addition to that, one of the more well-researched avenues to begin to change the neural networks in a traumatized brain is through the disclosure and active talking-about of our experiences and emotions.

What happens to us when we "find our voice" and actively share our stories? Empirical studies[21] done on the brain have demonstrated, at least on a cursory level, that consciously disclosing our thoughts and feelings about deeply personally meaningful experiences can have a positive effect on our physical and psychological well-being judged on a long-term scale. The benefits of this type of active disclosure are to be found in many areas: When we talk about our lives, we exert control over the words we use, the perspective we take, and the feelings we ascribe to it. When we talk about events in our lives, we are taking ownership over the things that make us feel powerless; we are given the opportunity to regulate the emotions that could otherwise seem beyond our ability to rein in.

But it is more than that. Verbally reexperiencing previous traumas and sources of stress in our past allows the formerly explicit amygdala-based memory to be recoded in the brain in a different area of the brain, the neocortex. The neocortex is the part of the brain in charge of declarative memory, or working memory, and these memories can then be deliberately accessed and controlled. The words we use and the language we adopt to talk about our experiences can help remove the emotions from our brain circuitry that works without our conscious thought and place them in another area, the neocortex, where we can exert our own control over it.

So, when I share my life with audiences, I am deliberate in the words I choose and the ideas I present. In years past, before I knew how to talk about my life and before I knew how to be disabled, I spoke like someone who was afraid, like someone whose life and events dictated the way she interpreted her very value or position in the world. This is not uncommon and, in fact, happens to many who have undergone life-changing events. These events become all-encompassing, omnipresent, or present when we do not choose them to be. The "finding of our voice" is not the finding of something that has been lost, it is the recapturing of our ideas. It is the reestablishment of our own sense of efficacy in our lives. It is the redefinition of ourselves as ourselves not as someone, something, or some time else. That ability is a human gift.

FROM PUBLIC SPEAKING TO PUBLIC SERVICE

Serving as a public speaker brought me closer to people I otherwise would not have known, as well as to sides of myself I also might not have ever known. Who we are is inextricably linked to the stories we tell about ourselves, the narratives we develop about ourselves, and the ways we choose to articulate them. Throughout each speech or public presentation I gave, I spoke with earnestness and sincerity about my belief in not only *our individual capacity to tackle challenges present in our lives* but also in the importance of *never underestimating our ability to effectuate change in the world*. As a public speaker, I would profess these things, but as the months following my graduation went on, it was becoming more obvious to me that, while I could claim some competency in the former, I had far less command of the latter. There were things I wanted to do and messages I wanted to convey that existed beyond the experiences I already had. I had seen how obstacles in my life and the lives of others could easily leave people feeling hopeless, ineffectual, and like challenge was identity-defining. But what I saw taking place on an individual level, I also saw taking place on a collective level. I saw a world that was still ready to deny opportunity rather than provide it. I saw a world that was unfriendly to many, especially those most in need of friends, and a world that was built on a structure that fundamentally put people on unequal footing. I saw a world that needed to change but I didn't have the first idea how I might be able to change it.

I was giving speeches, reminding people about their ability to effectuate change in the world, but, at the same time, did not always feel like I was making the change I, myself, wanted to make. It was as a result of this concern that I entered the Harvard Kennedy School of Government two years after I thought I had left Harvard forever. The Harvard Kennedy School (HKS) sits on a picturesque plot of land on the banks of the Charles River amidst all the legendary Harvard undergraduate houses. In some ways, the Harvard Kennedy School is a cross-river, publicly oriented response to the Harvard Business School, which sits on the opposing side of the river, yet there is a great deal of collaboration between the two. HKS, at least when I was a student there, housed an array of educational and professional opportunities for the civic-minded, the politically ambitious, the policy wonks, and the socially conscious. It is a haven for people who view the world as theirs for the changing.

The Master in Public Policy (MPP) program I was accepted into is generalist in nature, allowing people to specialize in areas like national security, business and government, science policy, nonprofit organization, political communications, foreign policy, social policy, health policy, and leadership. Since HKS was founded in 1936, interest in these areas, particularly over the past decade, has grown and so, too, has the institution itself. I entered HKS in 2002, the first admissions cycle following the attacks of September 11, a time within U.S. history characterized by its uncertainty, complexity, fear, and uneasiness. As a nation, we were undergoing all the emotions that we, as individuals, experience after undergoing trauma. I wanted to be part of the process by which we, as a nation, found our way through it.

Given the size of the 2002 MPP class, we were divided into four cohorts: Alpha, Beta, Gamma, and Delta, and students in each particular cohort were assigned to the same classes for the first semester. I was assigned to the Delta cohort, and true to the political nerdiness that pervaded the school, we called ourselves "the agents of change." Our class was as diverse in its background as it was in its interests, as motivated to improve the world as it was to improve one another. Each of us was there to gain the training necessary to enter a world of public service—nonprofit work, campaign work, political consulting, organizational consulting, foreign policy, diplomacy, and fields that are less easily categorized. Many of our classes at the Harvard Kennedy School were quintessentially and stereotypically Harvard—held in front of large lecture halls, where each student sat behind a placard bearing his or her name, so that the likelihood of being unexpectedly called on applied equally to everyone. It could be looked at as intimidating or thrilling, depending on your command of the material. Many of the courses demanded something more than mere textbook content. Many of the courses challenged students to integrate material across disciplines and apply it to real-world problems, as these global challenges were just as multifaceted and in need of cross-discipline solutions. As a society, it is impossible to effectively manage the catastrophic nature of climate change without also talking about international development, human rights, persuasion, and corporate social responsibility. It is impossible to discuss national security without also talking about the effects of globalization, nuclear nonproliferation, and access to resources. HKS encouraged us to become experts in isolated fields but also to understand how seemingly diverse or unrelated issues were inseparable from one another. There we were encouraged to think narrowly and broadly, vertically and horizontally. We were encouraged to do more, be more, and be unafraid in doing it.

I spent two years learning about domestic and foreign policy, reading political philosophy, learning the skills of negotiation and the art of leadership. I heard speakers from all parts of the world and all backgrounds, coming to share thoughts at the John F. Kennedy Jr. Forum at the Harvard University Institute of Politics. I met people who would change my life and my way of thinking, forever. And in those two years, I would see a side of myself that I never knew existed. But I still had to learn how to translate that into something meaningful.

I graduated from the Harvard Kennedy School teeming with ideas and possibility. At graduation, I gave one of the commencement speeches, which included these thoughts:

> *You, here, are among some of the brightest and fastest rising stars that can be gathered in one place. It is almost certain that many of you will seize upon the chances that have been laid before you and will leave the crimson walls of Harvard with a renewed sense of drive and purpose. Yet, the possibilities that await are only significant to the extent that we can view them as collective, and not individual, opportunities. With ability comes responsibility, a responsibility not only to personal achievement but to global progress. There are problems to be addressed and challenges to be faced that not one of us can confront alone, no matter who we are or what our potential might be; there is a shared responsibility that we have for one another, not only for those we call friends but also for those to whom we do not give the same title. For the benefit we derive for people, collectively, we also derive for ourselves, individually.*

Just like I am unable to move without the assistance of others, the world cannot move forward without our cooperation.

When I spoke those words to my graduating class, I did not know how much I was, in fact, speaking to myself. Leave the comfort and protection of Harvard's halls, all that you have learned and all of the resources you have, find the thing you care about, and do something to change it for the better. That was the charge I was posing to my classmates, but it was also the charge I needed to give to myself. When I left campus in May 2004, I had learned the lessons I needed to not only look within myself for things to change and improve upon, but also to look outside myself. When I left the Harvard Kennedy School campus, I had found my voice and understood how I wanted to use it.

It has been said, and rightly so, that if you want to run for public office, you should have a reason to do it. You need to give people a reason why they should give their vote to you, a reason why you care about the office you are seeking, and why your vision for how the world might look resonates with the concerns they have. This one, seminal task sounds simple. "Why are you running for office?" If you decide to run for office and you do not have a relatable, succinct, and easily understood response to this question, then you might as well stop before you even start. Politics, when done properly, is an arduous and demanding endeavor to pursue—it can eat at your soul and tear your heart out. But if you can clearly understand and then clearly articulate how your desire to serve the public can bring about a future from which many may benefit and that your contribution to that future is unique, you have cleared the first and, in some ways, biggest hurdle.

After earning my master's degree, I had a sense of purpose—a sense of resolve to impact the world in some positive way. At the same time, the Kennedy School bestowed on me an understanding of the multidimensional ways that a vision for the future is complicated by conflicting challenges, diverse interests, competing ideas, and irreconcilable solutions. I wanted to interweave this new knowledge with knowledge I had already gained through the events in my life. I had seen the inner workings of the health-care industry and had been a heralded example of medicine practiced at its best. I wanted to ensure that everyone who needed care could have access to it in the same way that I did and could avoid some of the battles that my family and I had been forced to take on. Having graduated from Harvard with my undergraduate and master's degrees, under the most unlikely circumstances, I had seen how education was a critical component to childhood development and was the vehicle by which people could transform their lives and engage in making a difference. I wanted to ensure that all children could be afforded the same chances I was, irrespective of where they may have come from. Returning to Long Island as a young adult out of college and graduate school, I had seen how the ways in which Long Island had been developed over the years—designed in such a notoriously ruthless way as to marginalize people from diverse racial and ethnic backgrounds and keep them off of Long Island—were now putting housing costs and transportation beyond reach for young families and young talent, thus impeding its growth. And I had seen how stem cell research could be the avenue to treatments and therapies unlike any we had seen before, and that it was within individual states' capabilities to fund this work if it had the will and understanding to do it.

These issues represented the platform on which I built my campaign. But a campaign needs to be more than just a summation of the planks on which it is built. A campaign, or, better said, a quest to serve in public office, needs to tell a story—it needs to tell *the* story about why the candidate's vision for the future is the right one, and why the candidate is the right person to help bring that future into existence.

My campaign was about looking at the challenges facing our world and communities today—whether from the perspective of being adequately prepared to meet the changes that our future will require or being able to better care for those who live right now—and how we were avoiding doing the real, difficult work required to solve them. As I would come to say countless times throughout the course of the eighteen months I spent on the campaign trail, I had seen enormous challenges in my own life and sought ways to overcome them. This attitude and way of being had become so central to my identity—so inextricably linked to how I understood myself at that time—that I wanted to use those learned skills and practiced talents to help New York and New Yorkers overcome some of the challenges they were experiencing. In some ways, especially for someone only twenty-seven years old, this was a lofty and possibly even grandiose idea. And I knew that. But in other ways, it was not either of those things at all. While policymaking, consensus building, and decision-making fundamentally require compromise and collaboration—the very functionalist ethics framework that underlies politics—they also require a willingness to see any problem from all of its vantage points and be unafraid in working toward its solution. Politics, as far as I understood and continue to understand it, requires the very same creativity, diversity in thinking, and unwavering hopefulness that living a life of challenge forces you to rely on every single day. That was the purpose behind my campaign. That was the story I wanted to tell.

As anyone with even the slightest political experience can attest, the vision and theory of politics resembles nearly none of the practicalities of it. We can envision great orators and statesmen whose words and deeds change the trajectory of history, but none of them arrived at his (and far more rarely her) bully pulpit without undergoing the tactics of a campaign. Though anyone can and should be able to accomplish them, there are steps to be taken and procedures to be followed in order to initiate a campaign for public office. There is a chain of command to be followed, a hierarchy of individuals to be spoken to in order for the path to be forged. Stepping away from a PhD program in political science that I had begun, I was ready to embark on my own path toward the ballot.

In August 2005, I visited the New York State Capitol building. After speaking with my family, talking about the possibility of running for office, explaining my rationale for doing so, I was ready—full of ideas, full of promise, full of enthusiasm. Running for office is not something to be taken lightly or frivolously. For me, it was a serious matter with potential that could take me in countless directions. At the New York State Capitol building, I spoke in depth with the then New York State Senate minority leader, David Paterson; toured the New York State Senate chambers; and was brought up to speed on bizarre myths and facts of the building. The experience was beautiful in appearance and thrilling in possibility. Over coffee and cookies in his office, Senator Paterson said to me, with the same look of possibility on his face, "Well, if you're serious about this and want to run, I will support you in every way I can. It's going to be a hard fight, but you have what it takes to fight it." Senator Paterson, himself, lived with a disability—he was born blind—and he was a no-nonsense disciple of working hard to get to where you want to be. "I know what it's like to run for office, and to run with a disability. It ain't easy, but it also ain't impossible."

My parents and I drove home from Albany to Long Island in what was one of the most ferocious thunderstorms I had ever seen. The sky was almost perpetually alight with bolts of lightning—two, three, four at a time—electrifying the sky. There was a point when, traveling south on the New York State Thruway, the rain was so heavy and the visibility so poor that we had to pull over, almost certain that we wouldn't make it home.

But amidst flashes of lightning and deluges of rain, I began to think about whether the decision to pursue public office was the right choice and about the details of what I knew would be one of the most significant endeavors I would undertake. And I thought about the simple but pristine, true words: "It ain't easy, but it also ain't impossible." Those words brought into articulation that which so much of my life had come to be— not easy but also not impossible, a test of strength but not an impassable one, an opportunity to reach inside myself and discover who I am when odds—whether taken willingly or by circumstance—are steep.

For eighteen months, during what was one of the most emotionally grueling yet exhilarating experiences I have willingly undertaken, my campaign manager and I worked side by side, morning until late at night. We had matching desks that sat next to one another in the sunroom of my home, and all day long, every day, we worked until we could not work anymore. I spent eighteen months planning and attending meetings with union representatives and community organizations—hearing their stories and learning about their unique concerns that were going unaddressed. I planned house parties and fundraisers and spent hours and hours each day making phone calls to potential donors so that I had the resources to ensure that the message I wanted to send was the message that people were receiving. I went to committee meetings, took part in debates, scheduled press conferences, and knocked on every door I could throughout the heart of Long Island.

As has been the case with nearly everything I've done in my life, my political campaign for New York State Senate was unconventional. My campaign had to be run in a manner entirely different from nearly any other because my candidacy was entirely different from nearly any other. To be sure, when living with a disability, every aspect of your day, and therefore your campaign, must be thought about differently and must take into consideration more potential difficulties than nondisabled candidates ever account for. There are daily impediments and personal, health-care, or circumstantial obstacles that can make a political campaign that much more challenging but, undoubtedly, that much more satisfying.

Running for office requires meeting people—meeting voters—many of whom are best found in their own homes and neighborhoods. As a candidate, I would travel with a team of volunteers to help knock on doors. Like homes across the country, many homes on Long Island had steps to the doorway that were inaccessible for me, not by distance but by design. To overcome this challenge, my campaign team and I devised a strategy through which one or several of the campaign volunteers would do the physical work of knocking on the doors, explaining that I was a candidate for office looking to introduce myself, and inviting the homeowner to come to talk to me. Over the course of many months and many knocked doors, I spoke to people of all backgrounds—all races, ethnicities, political ideologies, socioeconomic statuses—and the concerns from home to home, community to community, were often very much the same, though the path to solving these concerns might differ. I would attend speeches and press events with my own stand and microphone, knowing that podiums often could not accommodate wheelchairs. I always had to be prepared to answer the consistent question, "Are you physically able to be a politician?" I knew that I was not only physically able, but by virtue of the skills that are developed and sharpened through living life with disability, I was as mentally, emotionally, and intellectually able as anyone pursuing office could be. These are skills you learn, manifestations of creativity you employ, and questions you answer by the doing, not simply the saying.

None of this was unexpected, even after Senator Paterson advised me to expect it. But in addition to the shared vision I wanted to convey, I knew there was another statement I was making by choosing to run for office. There are social conditions that foster exclusion and perpetuate biases of what our legislators should look like and who our decision-makers ought to be. This is ultimately to everyone's detriment, as better and more comprehensive solutions to complex problems are much more likely to develop when they incorporate diverse experiences and ways of life—that is the moral imperative and practical rationale behind inclusion. When it comes to politics and the image of our legislators, people with disabilities almost never are among those we envision. I wanted to help change this. I wanted to help each child with a disability envision a county legislature or the halls of Congress with him in it.

Abraham Lincoln touted, in his Gettysburg Address, a U.S. government "of the people, by the people, for the people," but regrettably, this vision has not been operationalized for all the people. According to the 2018 Disability Status Report,[22] 12.6 percent of the U.S. population lives with a disability—some 42 million people. These numbers are on a steady rise, as the population ages and as medical advances allow people to live longer and healthier lives following the onset of disability or injury. According to a report issued by Rutgers' Program for Disability Research, in 2020, it was estimated that 67.7 million voters either had or lived with someone who had a disability.[23] Yet despite the immensity of these numbers, people with disabilities are vastly underrepresented in elected office, at all levels. The National Council on Independent Living, a nonprofit advocacy and disability-rights organization, tracked the number of candidates with disabilities running in the 2018 federal elections. According to their open source database[24]—which they admit may not be fully complete given a societal reluctance to disclose a disability—only eleven candidates with a disability were running for either U.S. House of Representatives or U.S. Senate. Of these, five either dropped out or lost in a primary. This is a mere 2.3 percent of the 470 congressional seats open, and it is only one-sixth the proportion of their representation in general society.

While it is troubling enough that our legislators do not look like the general population, this is exacerbated by the fact that people with disabilities are often much more marginally affected by the results of many of the policy measures that are debated in congressional chambers. Critical and hotly contested issues like cuts to Social Security Disability Insurance and Supplemental Security Income; cuts to Medicaid and Medicare; the elimination of independent living programs; cuts to biomedical research; the growth of a national paid family medical leave plan; funding for the Individuals with Disabilities Education Act; support for the Supplemental Nutrition Assistance Program—these are not mere political arguments for people with disabilities, but matters of life and death. The disability-rights movement began with the rallying cry "Nothing about us without us," which has now been modified to the more accurate "Nothing without us," and this implies that decisions regarding the lives and welfare of people with disabilities should not be made without the consultation of disabled people themselves. What more influential position than legislators to contribute to these conversations?

It has long been demonstrated, empirically and anecdotally,[25] that organizations and decision-makers regularly make better and more comprehensive decisions when a diversity of voices is included. For too long, in most aspects of society, but in politics quite particularly, inclusion of diverse voices and points of view has not meant the inclusion of people with disabilities. This is not true inclusion; it is inclusion à la carte. This is also despite the fact that people with disabilities are often forced by circumstance to adopt the types of leadership, creativity, problem-solving, and resilience skills that excellence in elected office demands. Even in 2006, I knew these facts to be true, and I knew that they needed to change. I wanted to be part of making that change.

My campaign team and I had eighteen months that were more purposeful and transformative than I ever really previously imagined such a short timeframe could be, and the memories that I have of that time are silhouetted by richness and depth. Friends from college and graduate school became involved. Family members knocked on doors and made fundraising phone calls. Community members put up signs and hosted house parties. In essence, it was like a homecoming—a giving back to my community all that it had given to me.

Election Day 2006 is a day so deeply infused with emotion and intensity that some of my memories of it are scant. After having spent the previous weeks working to get out the vote, my campaign team—campaign manager, finance director, door knockers, sign hangers, phone callers—and I all were running purely off of spirit and pride in what we had accomplished. The campaign had been endorsed by *The New York Times*, was covered on the *Today* show, and had generated much more attention and required many more resources for my opponent than anyone had initially anticipated. On the night of Election Day, I joined my fellow Long Island Democratic candidates at a results-watching party. The results that I watched, though, did not return in my favor. Despite all of the hard work, all of the ideas I had to make Long Island a richer and stronger place to live, and all of the integrity and decency with which

I believe the campaign was run, I was not victorious. At least not in an electoral sense.

After the election was over, I felt despondent and lost. I felt like the road I had taken to make the change I felt the world needed had hit a dead end, and I was at a loss for how to position myself next. I knew how hard we all had worked and the virtue of what we were trying to achieve, and I wanted to see those efforts turn into realities. I wanted to be given the chance to make the difference I knew I could make. It was heartbreaking. Nevertheless, there is not a single thing about my campaign that I regret or would change. It was grueling, it was exhausting, it was deeply personal, and it was a reflection of all that I know policymaking and leadership to be. In a way that is perhaps different from many political campaigns, my campaign was one that resembled the strongest parts of me, and those parts were made aware to many, myself included.

The interesting thing about change is that it is fairly agnostic with respect to what form it takes and from what source it comes. It is the work that is of essence—the actual *doing* that can tackle challenges and bring about a world that is more just. This mechanism for action or mobilization for change is not contingent on a title that is held or position that is occupied. The work is in the doing. So often, we ascribe *leadership* to a position or to a particular person, but I had forgotten one of the most fundamental lessons I had learned and one of the most valuable gifts I had ever been given: the knowledge that leadership isn't something you *are*, it is something you *do*, and something you can do from *anywhere*. We can become infatuated with titles, intoxicated by the thoughts of power that they encompass, but leadership is an entity of an entirely different sort. Leadership exists wherever there is work to be done. In essence, leadership exists everywhere when we have the imagination to identify it and the will and allies to do it.

I am often asked if I would ever consider running for office again, and my answer is always the same: that if I were to run again, it would have to be because my potential position would put me in a better place to effectuate meaningful change for people than wherever I might be at the time—and not for any self-aggrandizing or attention-seeking reason, which can easily be the case when your primary charge as a candidate is to convince everyone how terrific you are. But it is not something I would either rule out or take on frivolously. The good you do is done no matter where you do it, as long as you do it. The challenges you are willing to take on can be taken on no matter which side of the legislature walls your office may reside. The lives you change and the difference you make are there to be changed and made whether you are knocking on a door or opening one.

*Top: Brooke and her parents with director Christopher Reeve
and the cast of* The Brooke Ellison Story. *Left to right:
Lacey Chabert; Brooke's mother, Jean; Mary Elizabeth
Mastrantonio; Brooke's father, Ed; and John Slattery.
Bottom: Reeve and Brooke on set in New Orleans, July 2004.
(Photo by Diana DeRosa)*

9

←——————→

REGENERATION

We often refrain from difficult conversations that force us to either challenge or defend our beliefs, and as a result, we can often miss opportunities to learn or teach.

JUST AS HOPE CAN BECOME part of your identity—part of the way you understand yourself and your relation to the world—so, too, can leadership. Once leadership and change making become lenses through which you view the world, they remain the frame through which you view the world. Hope and leadership are two versions of the same lens through which we view our lives. They become part of us—part of the very core of our being. You become the change maker. You become a vehicle for hope.

For many years of my life, I knew there was an implicit disadvantage that was embedded in living with a disability. I knew this in the way that everyone, essentially, knows this: that it is simply part of reality. But as I grew older and became more self-aware, I became more conscious of the unfairness of this assumption. The injustice of it. The unacceptable nature of it. People with disabilities could be blind, but they did not need to be invisible. People with disabilities could be deaf, but their voices and their needs do not need to go unheard. People with disabilities could be seated in wheelchairs, but they did not need to be denied a seat at the table. Yet this was the reality I was seeing far too frequently: people with disabilities entirely absent from boardrooms, absent from positions of leadership, absent from conversations and decision-making related to important social issues, even ones that directly impacted their lives. This was the power imbalance that needed to be rectified. This was the work I wanted to do.

Following my state senate run, I remained involved in political circles, but I needed a more stable future that could also allow me to be a part of the changes that I still wanted to see made in the world. One of the most tangible ways that I stayed involved in politics was through my appointment to the Ethics Committee of the newly formed Empire State Stem Cell Board. During my campaign, stem cell research and the importance of providing public funds to this research was a central plank in my platform. The federal government had put stringent restrictions on funding for embryonic stem cell research, and as the U.S. federal government is the biggest and most significant funder of science in the world, this fact was severely hampering efforts being made by biomedical scientists to develop treatments and cures to some of humanity's most devastating diseases and conditions.

I had become involved in and passionate about advances in biomedical research very shortly after my accident. Newly elected, President Bill Clinton had signed legislation that would broaden availability for materials and tissues on which to conduct research for diseases and conditions like spinal cord injury. Newly injured, I had become disabled and did not want to be anymore. I had endured an injury and I wanted it repaired. I saw all the things in my life that I had lost, and I wanted to regain them. I wanted to breathe without a ventilator. I wanted to move without a wheelchair. I wanted to be fixed. I wanted to be cured.

Within the disability community, talking about things like "treatments," "cures," and "therapies" is fraught with potential controversy, controversy that I have found myself in the thick of. The implication that there is something that needs to be "fixed" within people with disabilities is, for many, troubling, if not denigrating. For some people within the disability community, a focus on things like "cures" or "treatments" to the physical conditions that cause disability is tantamount to saying that there is something wrong with these people, something that society would be better without. According to others in the disability community, looking at disability in this framework bolsters a medical model of disability, in which disability is viewed as a medical or physical failure rather than something that is more deeply embedded in social factors like our built environments and matters of public policy. If we believe disability to be a naturally occurring aspect of the human experience, then there should be no need to "cure" it. It would be as commonplace and non-noteworthy as living life with red hair or a French accent. But corollary to this belief has to be a set of public policies and societal constructs that make the lives of people with disabilities as rich and as fully integrated as anyone else's. That's simply not the case.

Particularly for those who experience disability on a noncongenital basis, for instance from an injury or disease, the inclination is to want to have the injury healed or the disease cured. That is the fundamental logic behind most biomedical inquiry—to treat disease and to reduce the burden of injury so that our bodies can be restored to the most "healthy" state possible and, therefore, we can live as rich and full a life as we so desire. As with a broken ankle or a bout of pneumonia, we want to be treated and return to life as we had known it. For some people with disabilities, this is an inappropriate way to view disability—that understanding disability to be a physical failure placed within a medical context results in serious, detrimental implications on how they are perceived within society and how they feel about their lives.

I am a woman with a disability, but I am also a woman who is actively and vehemently pro-cures and pro-treatments. I am also pro-disability, or, better said, a tireless fighter on behalf of the rights of people with disabilities, working to help reduce the sociocultural parts of our world that make people more or less *disabled*. Over the years, on a variety of fronts, I have dedicated myself to the full spectrum of disability: the curative and treatment side on the one hand, and the policy and participation side on the other. I don't view these ideas as mutually exclusive but, rather, collectively exhaustive—a full range of ideas that I have associated with disability, none of which is more disability-friendly than the other.

The fact of the matter is that, for many disabilities, there are real and painful losses that are experienced by virtue of the disability. Some of these are the result of practical and societal shortcomings that have failed to meet the needs of people with disabilities, and others of these are physical or health-related in nature. Both of these types of losses can diminish quality of life so much that people with disabilities might prefer a life lived without disability. There are comorbidities, or accompanying physical conditions, that subject individuals to decreased quality of life and lower life expectancy. For people with spinal cord injuries, they can be plentiful—increased risk of heart disease, increased risk of obesity, increased risk of type 2 diabetes, increased risk of kidney stones, increased risk of respiratory infection and urinary tract infection, untreatable pressure ulcers, musculoskeletal atrophy, and physical injury. These correlating conditions can sometimes be devastating and are often extremely difficult. A pursuit to treat or cure disability is based in a desire to treat and cure these comorbidities, to reduce the pain and suffering that individuals have to experience due to circumstances beyond their control.

This pursuit for treatment and cures can take place in tandem with the kinds of policy changes and societal changes that must be made to increase quality of life for people with disabilities. It is possible to want to address the physical pain and suffering that some people with disabilities experience while, at the same time, to want to address things like access to employment or education or social participation that can also impact quality of life. One is not in lieu of the other. Working on both fronts at the same time provides people with the greatest number of opportunities to live their lives as they so choose. That is how I have understood my position, as both an advocate and activist in the realm of stem cell research and as an advocate and activist in the realm of disability.

Though I have come to understand my position to be at this intersection, there are many others who have not arrived at this position and have been quite vocal about their difference in opinion. Regrettably, given my advocacy on both fronts, there have been some within the disability sphere who have been quite critical of me and others who have advocated for a similar approach. While I have willingly subjected myself to avenues of criticism or difference of opinion by virtue of my involvement in politics and other arenas, this criticism I have found to be among the most disheartening and most unexpected. I don't endure this criticism alone, though, and many of my closest friends within the disability circles, in their pursuits of treatment and cures, have experienced the same thing. Most notable among these friends was actor, activist, and friend Christopher Reeve.

It was shortly after my graduation from Harvard in 2000 that Chris and I first met. He had read about my graduation in *The New York Times*.

The phone rang at my house one summer afternoon with someone on the other end requesting to speak with me. "I have Christopher Reeve here to speak with you, can I patch you through?" My feeling of shock to that question was only outdone by the question that Chris, himself, asked of me. In our conversation, Chris mentioned that he had wanted to tell the life story of someone who lived with circumstances similar to his own—someone living with quadriplegia and on a ventilator. He asked me if he could tell my story, in the form of a movie that he would direct and produce. There are few, if any, moments in most lives that produce the precise constellation of emotions I felt upon being asked that question. I was honored but unsure, excited but afraid, ready to go but without any idea of what steps might be required. Chris and his team of colleagues and caregivers came to my home in Stony Brook a few weeks later to talk about the details, in what was, in more ways than one, an utterly other-worldly experience. Over the course of a four-hour conversation around my kitchen table, *The Brooke Ellison Story*, the film based on my book, *Miracles Happen*, was brought to life.

It would not be until nearly four years later that all of the pieces would be put into place in order for the film to be developed. Over the summer of 2004, *The Brooke Ellison Story* was filmed in New Orleans through a process that, despite my very limited exposure to filmmaking, I suspect was much more familial and took on a deeper significance than the production of most other movies. My parents and I drove down to New Orleans from Long Island. Kysten and Reed both flew down to New Orleans several days later, and we all spent nearly a month in the hot but spectacular New Orleans South, watching our lives become *The Brooke Ellison Story*. Chris's wife, Dana, and children were on-set throughout the filming. Members of the cast and crew brought their families down to New Orleans to be a part of the process and to watch it unfold. Sets were designed to look like my childhood home, my community, my college dorm room, like scenes of my life were drawing me back in to be lived again.

The Brooke Ellison Story was, quite obviously, a very personal experience for me but also for those whose lives were not being told. Chris passed away just two weeks before *The Brooke Ellison Story* was scheduled to premiere on television, making an already intensely emotional experience that much more so. Every telling of the story of *The Brooke Ellison Story* necessarily—and thankfully—is a story that includes my friendship with Christopher Reeve. Every time *The Brooke Ellison Story* is aired on television, which it still is to this day all over the world, I am contacted by people who I would only know because of Chris. Our friendship was born out of experiences that very few ever undergo. Though our lives were vastly different circumstantially, they were forged together through common struggles, common losses, and in hopes for the future.

Through his research foundation, the Christopher and Dana Reeve Foundation, Chris indefatigably and doggedly sought a cure for spinal cord injury, one that would allow him and others with spinal cord injury to return to their lives as they had known them. To many, myself included, Chris was a visionary in the true sense of the word, seeing an outcome that could positively impact many lives and using all his resources and connections to realize that outcome. He was brave in many ways that people never have to be brave; he was committed to causes that few people ever commit themselves to; he took action in all the ways that action could be taken; and he spoke on behalf of many who needed their circumstances spoken for. Chris was a hero and an icon to many, but like me and others staunchly advocating for biomedical research and cures for disease and disability, Chris sometimes became the target of those who did not agree with that outcome or with the path needed to get there.

←———→

Just like talking about "cures" in the context of disability is fraught with controversy, so, too, are some of the trajectories of biomedical research being pursued to achieve these cures. Historically speaking, few avenues of biomedical research have received as much political and social scrutiny as has the field of stem cell research. Particularly at the turn of the twenty-first century, stem cell research existed—and continues to exist—as one of the most exciting areas of biomedicine to be found, with the potential to change the way medicine is practiced and the ways through which medicine will ultimately treat some of the most devastating diseases and conditions facing humanity. Nevertheless, despite the promise and potential of this field of research, it has been mired in social and political discord that has hampered its progression and has sometimes put its future in question. While some of this discord is based in deeply established political or moral beliefs, much more of it is based in misunderstanding and scientific misinformation.

There is a great deal of uncertainty about what stem cell research involves, what potential it has, depending on a host of factors, and even how the practice of science research is conducted. In its simplest terms, a "stem cell" is a unique type of cell found in the human body, in its organs and bone marrow, in a newly fertilized egg, in umbilical cord blood, or in the placenta, that has the unique capability to divide infinitely—a process called self-renewal—and to develop, or specialize, into other types of cells found in the body. What does this mean, exactly? Cells in our body—of which there are trillions—are given a distinct set of instructions regarding which genes they should express and, thus, what functions they should perform to help keep us alive. However, not all stem cells are created equal, and they fall into the classes of "adult stem cells" and "embryonic stem cells," each having its own characteristics. Adult stem cells, which were discovered in the 1950s, comprise the stem cells found in organs, bone marrow, and umbilical cord blood. Though the use of these cells in existing treatments is well-documented, adult stem cells are limited in their potentiality to differentiate into the two hundred types of cells in the human body and, as a result, are largely restricted in their applicability for treatment. Embryonic stem cells, however, are universal in their ability to become other types of cells in the human body. They are both the blank slate and gold standard in the stem cell field. Though not yet harnessed, the expected future applications resulting from research on embryonic stem cells are vast, ranging from the potential to generate replacement cells for those lost in disease or injury to the creation of cellular media on which to test drug efficacy.

Why would something like this be useful? When many of us experience disease or disability, something either goes awry in our cells and they can no longer develop correctly, or our cells are damaged beyond repair. The hope of stem cell research is that when tissues are damaged in disease or disability, they can be treated, repaired, or replaced through materials prepared with the use of stem cells. As the field has grown and evolved, applications for the use of stem cells in the treatment and research of disease and disability have, likewise, grown to avenues never expected, including the development of tissues and cell cultures that have disease embedded within them. These scientifically engineered tissue samples can then be the sites on which to test potential medications and can allow scientists to watch disease develop to see what transpires or goes wrong when it does.

The potential usage of stem cells to treat disease and disability is enormous, and, particularly when the field was early in its development, there were several diseases and disabilities that were broadly discussed as being particularly strong candidates for therapies derived from stem cell research. Spinal cord injury was one of these, and in no small way attributable to Chris and his efforts. But, like all work, stem cell research needed funding to advance—funds that scientists across the country use to purchase their materials, pay graduate students, and ultimately make the breakthroughs that carry society forward. Historically, the biggest funder of science has been the U.S. government. However, particularly in the early years of the twenty-first century, there were sharp ethical disagreements surrounding this research that took prominence over the promise of the science itself. At the time, much attention was being placed on embryonic stem cells: stem cells that are derived from the inner cell mass of newly fertilized embryos. The derivation of these stem cells results in the termination of the embryo, a process which some felt was not ethically sound. In response to this concern, scientists, science advocates, patients, and patient advocates argued that the embryos from which these stem cells are derived are, in fact, left over from in vitro fertilization attempts; in essence, they are unused and kept in cryopreservation and would be discarded anyway. Why not put them to valuable, humanitarian and biomedical use, in a way that could potentially revolutionize medicine? At the time when these debates were taking place, President George W. Bush was seated in the White House, and he was in alignment with those in opposition to the advancement of this science. Despite the potential that this research held, and continues to hold, for the future of medical treatments, under the Bush administration, restrictions were placed on this work in a way that impeded its progression.

It is rare that the U.S. government does not fund basic exploratory science, the kind of research that lays the groundwork for fundamental understandings and societal progress. Whether it's biomedical research, environmental research, energy research, or any other type, this funding is typically provided by agencies in the federal government—the National Science Foundation, the National Institutes of Health, the Department of Defense. These agencies provide money for science research because science is understood to be a "public good" or, in other words, a pursuit that is of benefit to everyone. The U.S. government provides the kind of coordination and prioritization needed to allow innovation to grow and research to take place in a well-overseen manner. Because of the strong and severely limiting restrictions being put on the funding available to stem cell research by the federal government, and because the research was thought to be so important to the future of medicine, individual states, like California, Massachusetts, and others, were attempting to fill this gap in funding by implementing their own stem cell funding initiatives. California's Proposition 71, which established the $3 billion bond initiative funding the California Institute for Regenerative Medicine, was the biggest and most noteworthy. My campaign for state senate called for similar efforts to be made in New York. The logic seemed obvious to me—not only could this research potentially be the groundwork for treatments and therapies to devastating diseases of many kinds, but it would also serve as a strong economic driver for the state of New York, possibly enticing the most brilliant and progressive scientists to come here to do their work.

During my campaign, I spoke at length about this work and about how stem cell research could serve as the basis of hope for not just New Yorkers but for people around the world. The idea of hope is one that we all want and need, especially when it is presented as something within our collective capacity to create and achieve—the use of human intellect and commitment to alleviate human suffering. The intertwining of stem cell research and hope was an intensely personal message but also a shared message, because, in essence, it was a representation of isolating difficult—and sometimes even heartbreaking—challenges and using our shared knowledge to reduce it. Our politics and our lives need more courage to view matters that way.

I wasn't the only candidate running for office in New York who felt that the state should create its own stem cell–funding initiatives. The leading candidates for governor and lieutenant governor, Eliot Spitzer and David Paterson, took this issue as an important avenue for the pursuit and expansion of New York's future and, with that in mind, incorporated it into their platform for the governor's race. Throughout the campaign season, we held several campaign events together, to talk about stem cell research and how New York ought to be on the forefront of it. We conducted press conferences and presentations with scientists at Cold Spring Harbor Laboratory, with physicians at New York hospitals, and with philanthropists at the New York Stem Cell Foundation to disseminate information and build support for the importance of this research. The efforts worked. Despite some of the controversy that had been generated around the research on a national level, there was strong support for this research being conducted in New York.

After Eliot Spitzer and David Paterson were successfully elected in 2006, one of the first initiatives they undertook was to create the Empire State Stem Cell Board, passed by both the New York State Assembly and New York State Senate, designed to provide funding to stem cell research projects in the state. The Empire State Stem Cell Board was to be composed of two separate committees: the Funding Committee, which would review grant applications and allocate funds to them, and the Ethics Committee, which would develop the parameters within which this research could be funded. The Funding Committee was to be composed of scientists and physicians with expertise in stem cell and regenerative science. The Ethics Committee, on the other hand, was to be composed of lawyers, scholars, ethicists, theologians, and community stakeholders with knowledge about the pressing questions surrounding the ethics of the field. Members of these committees would be chosen by the governor's office, as well as by the offices of the senate and assembly majority and minority leaders.

I was appointed to the Ethics Committee of the Empire State Stem Cell Board by Governor Spitzer's office, specifically by Lieutenant Governor Paterson. For years, I had been a staunch advocate for and researcher of stem cell science, but I had never delved deeply into the ethical questions that the field raised. I was twenty-eight years old—decades younger than anyone else on the committee—and unfamiliar with the nuances of ethical debate, but I was passionate and I represented a voice that would not otherwise be included in this conversation.

The first meeting of the Ethics Committee of the Empire State Stem Cell Board took place near the New York State Department of Health's New York City office, in downtown Manhattan. The building was in the financial district, overlooking the site of the World Trade Center, and from the penthouse meeting room, you could see for miles in every direction. The construction of what was then being called the Freedom Tower (now One World Trade Center) had already begun, and I remember thinking how much the country, the state of New York, and the lives of people living in both had changed so drastically in the years since 9/11. I remember wishing that instances of violence and heartache would start to give way to more instances of progress and hope.

The charge that was given to us as a committee was to explore the ethical questions surrounding stem cell research and then propose a policy that conformed to our ethical determinations on these questions, of which there were many. The prospect was intimidating, to be sure, and would involve consideration of some of the most hotly debated and socially divisive topics integrated into science. The meetings were open to the public and were also livestreamed on the New York State Department of Health website, to ensure the highest degree of transparency in our debates. The meetings were chaired by the New York State commissioner of health, Richard Daines.

All committee members were seated at a long arrangement of tables, put together in the shape of a horseshoe, with the board staff and leadership seated at the shortest side. I remember looking around at all the members of the committee and feeling as though I didn't belong. In the span of what seemed like minutes but was likely only fractions of a second, my brain executed both sides of an internal debate, starting with the notion that I was not adequately equipped to do the work we were charged to do and, thankfully, counterarguing that not a single person at the table could approach the issue of stem cell research from as personal or experiential a perspective as I could. I let that conviction carry me through all the upcoming discussions, debates, and intermittent times of doubt that were to come.

Over the course of what would be the next five years, the Ethics Committee of the Empire State Stem Cell Board would debate the ethics and permissibility of not simply embryonic stem cell research, but also the more nuanced yet equally ethically challenging policy intricacies that the research involved. I was joined on the committee by medical ethicists from universities and research institutions throughout the state, a Catholic priest who focused on ethical debates pertaining to the question of life, a friar and philosopher who did the same, a physician, and several lawyers with backgrounds in ethics. And then there was me. In one of the interventions I made over the years I served on the board, I stated straightforwardly and unabashedly that, although I would have liked to have believed that my selection to serve on the Ethics Committee was due to my policymaking experience in the field, in honesty, I knew that it was far more because of my life as a person who could conceivably benefit from the advances that this research might provide. But I wanted to—in fact, I needed to—play both roles, the role of the *patient*, whose lived experience was unique and valuable, and the role of the *expert*, who could present an important ethical argument. In many ways, these two roles were one and the same.

There are, and have always been, many ethical questions surrounding the advancement of science practice—questions regarding how scientists conduct themselves, questions regarding the protection of materials and subjects used in the scientific process, questions regarding the publication process, questions regarding the ownership of intellectual property involved in the research, and questions regarding how far we can push the boundaries of science while remaining morally comfortable. All these questions are asked in the field of stem cell research, but also many more. And it was all these questions that we, as a committee with members from vastly different perspectives, needed to come to a resolution on in order for stem cell research to be a possibility in New York.

I wouldn't consider myself to have been "at odds" with anyone on the committee, yet it didn't take many meetings or discussions to realize which committee members fell on what ideological sides of the arguments and who was somewhere in the middle. Preceding each meeting, our seats at the table were always prescribed for us, and almost invariably, I would find myself seated directly across from a committee member whose perspectives were staunchly different from my own.

The first debate we took on was whether or not embryonic stem cell research should even be permitted in New York, and if so, if our policy should permit the derivation of new embryonic stem cell lines. At that time, there were stem cell lines—in other words, embryonic stem cells and their progeny—already in existence, meaning they had already been extracted from an embryo and were being used by scientists for research. Some argued that these existing stem cell lines ought to be enough and that no more should be created. Scientists responded to this by arguing that the existing stem cell lines were not especially usable and lacked the kind of genetic diversity needed to ensure that scientific advances were available for everyone.

Other debates centered on whether the state of New York should provide research dollars to projects that involved the extraction of stem cells from existing, frozen embryos. These embryos, or, scientifically speaking, blastocysts, could be no greater than fourteen days into development, smaller than the tip of the needle, and would be composed of no more than several hundred cells. At this point in an embryo's development, most women do not know that they are pregnant, as they have not yet even missed a menstrual cycle, and it is not uncommon that embryos this early in development are naturally miscarried without anyone even being aware of it.

The first vote we took on this issue was crafted in such a way as to allow for some ongoing debate. The vote was whether to place a moratorium on the derivation of new embryonic stem cell lines until the committee had the time to debate, research, and learn more about the issue. The tensions surrounding the vote were high and the implications were considerable— on the one hand, a moratorium might provide enough time for certain committee members to become more comfortable with the permissibility of stem cell derivation, but on the other hand, a moratorium might find its way into becoming an outright prohibition. Much like the swing votes on the Supreme Court, those in the middle of the polarity points would be the ones to truly decide which direction we would take. It had only been several years since I had graduated from the Harvard Kennedy

School, and I had not anticipated seeing so many of the concepts and ideas we had discussed in leadership and negotiation—stakeholdership, alliance building, perspective taking, growing the pie, best alternative to a negotiated agreement (BATNA)[26]—to be a true part of my life so quickly. This was the work I had been trained to do, but much like calculus or rhyme scheme, they were not skills I thought I might ever be called to use.

The vote on a moratorium on the derivation of new embryonic stem cell lines, and therefore broaden the genetic diversity of research lines being used, was ultimately passed, meaning that, for an indeterminate amount of time, this process would not be permitted in New York. This was not the outcome I was hoping for, but it defined the landscape of what would lie ahead, as well as where the points of compromise and persuasion might exist.

Shortly after the moratorium was put into place, we voted to lift it at a subsequent board meeting. In the duration between the placement of the moratorium and the time it was lifted, the committee heard from scientists and ethicists who were deeply versed in this particular question. We heard from scientists at Harvard who had been fighting feverishly for years for avenues to open for research—scientists who founded the groundbreaking Harvard Stem Cell Institute. We heard from scientists and ethicists who had advised presidential administrations on the research, as well as policymakers from the California Institute for Regenerative Medicine, which had been created several years before. We heard about what ethical restrictions would be placed on this process and how the research was conducted under the greatest of care. We heard how the derivation of new embryonic stem cell lines was scientifically necessary, as the lines that were in existence were genetically limited and not reflective of the diversity of the U.S. population. We heard how the future of the field could not practically advance without this permissibility.

In the coming years, we would debate the structure of informed consent documents for couples looking to donate their "leftover" or, the more appropriate term, "supernumerary," embryos to research. These couples often would have undergone the in vitro fertilization process and would have embryos that they were not intending to use for the growth of their family. The informed consent document had to be clear and precise in terms of what couples were agreeing to and what they understood about it, so that there was never any misunderstanding. We would debate whether it would be ethically permissible to combine cells from different species for scientists to have access to cell types that could carry different diseases and genetic abnormalities. And, perhaps most heatedly, we debated whether New York would become the first place in the world to provide compensation to women who decided to donate their eggs to stem cell research.

Women being compensated for their eggs when they were used for reproduction was a common practice; all along the walls of Harvard University, presumably where one might find supposedly genetically desirable traits, there would be advertisements looking for women to donate their eggs to couples for artificial insemination. Yet when women wanted to donate their eggs purely for research, thinkers and policymakers had drawn the contradictory conclusion time and time again that this provision of money might entice women to undergo a procedure that could cause health complications. The logical argument behind this determination was that providing compensation to egg donors would disproportionately prey upon women of low socioeconomic means. The argument was then, presumably, that, simply because a woman was financially insecure, she was not capable of making proper decisions about her life.

In a vote that felt like something out of the U.S. Senate—full of argumentation on both sides and an audience packed wall-to-wall with scientists, advocates, clergy, and students—the Ethics Committee passed the first-ever policy that allowed New York State to compensate women who decided to donate their eggs to research. The compensation was to account for their time, effort, and willingness to subject themselves to discomfort through the donation process. As we had heard from Harvard scientists, this was a provision they had sought for many years. These researchers had attempted to recruit women to donate their eggs without compensation and successfully recruited exactly zero donors. Zero. This was groundbreaking policymaking, something that had never been done before but was of immense importance to the field. As a matter of fact, it was because of this very provision that some of the most groundbreaking advances in regenerative and biomedical research were made in New York. Using donated eggs, researchers at the New York Stem Cell Foundation were able to unlock the mysteries of mitochondrial disorders that are passed from mother to child and then find ways to circumvent that by transferring the nucleus of one egg to another. These were things that were previously unimaginable but made possible through policy and prudence.

My membership on the Ethics Committee had such an influence on me that it changed the entire trajectory of my life. I wanted to dig deeper into not just the ethical questions surrounding stem cell research, but the ethical questions surrounding science and medicine more generally. My life had given me expertise that could not be found in any textbook, but I wanted to match that with the knowledge that *was* contained in the textbooks, as well as the PhD degree to accompany it. I asked Dr. Daines, the New York State commissioner of health, who had since become a dear friend, to write a letter of recommendation on my behalf. I asked Jonathan Moreno, a renowned medical ethicist who had served several U.S. presidents and was an endowed professor at the University of Pennsylvania, to write a letter of recommendation on my behalf. And I asked Susan Solomon, philanthropic visionary and founder of the New York Stem Cell

Foundation, to write a letter of recommendation on my behalf. I knew there was a new phase of my life I wanted to seize and contributions I needed to make. By September 2009, I was ready to begin my PhD at Stony Brook University, studying the sociology of science and medicine.

I had, for many years, considered completing my education and entering academia, to contribute to knowledge and our understandings of the world. Right after I had completed my master in public policy at the Harvard Kennedy School, I had begun my PhD in political science. The time was not right for me, though. Almost without a lapse, I had been a student all my life, and I needed to experience something different, something outside of the classroom. I wanted and needed to act, not just study. In that timeframe, in addition to running for New York State Senate, I founded a nonprofit organization, The Brooke Ellison Project, which had as its mission to educate people on the science of and need for stem cell research. If I wasn't engaging in the research directly, I wanted to help level the path for scientists by correcting misrepresentations of what the science was all about. Working with filmmaker Jimmy Siegel, I created a documentary, entitled *Hope Deferred*, which told the stories of the lives of people whose daily struggle with disease and disability might be alleviated through advances in stem cell research. In the film, families spoke with passion and emotion about their lives, scientists spoke with passion and emotion about their work, and I spoke with passion and emotion about my commitment to both.

Hope Deferred had its premiere at The Times Center in New York City, with a live performance of a song, "Hold On," written by a dear friend purely for this film. The film was shown to audiences across the country—audiences of all kinds, including scientists, physicians, college students, and community members. It was entered in film festivals and was recognized for its humanitarian impact. But more than that, *Hope Deferred* allowed me to synthesize and unify two fields—disability and biomedical research—that were perhaps not communicating as well as they could. It was an opportunity to hear from the families of people experiencing disease and disability and what those experiences meant to them. It was an opportunity for people without disability to understand some of what it is like to live with disability and how people can and do suffer in ways that go beyond what can be solved through societal changes. It was an opportunity to expose people who may not have scientific background with the fundamentals of science and why scientists practice it. It was an opportunity for me to do meaningful work—work that required me to tackle a challenging societal issue and make change through it. And it was a restoration of hope for some of those who may have felt that it was lost.

In the years that I ran The Brooke Ellison Project, I learned how to maintain commitment and dedication to a cause with which not everyone agrees. Much of the work I had conducted until that point, political office seeking notwithstanding—revolved around issues like challenge and hope: issues for which there is generally little disagreement and even less controversy. This situation is rare. Entering into positions of advocacy or taking stands on complex issues almost inevitably requires you to not only confront opposing beliefs but also to confront the people who hold opposing beliefs, and this is by no means easy. We often refrain from difficult conversations that force us to either challenge or defend our beliefs, and as a result, we can often miss opportunities to learn or teach. Listening, discussing, learning, and growing—these are fundamental components to leadership, and we all have the capacity to demonstrate them if we find the will to do it.

By 2009, as the political landscape in which stem cell research was evolving was broadening, I was ready to make strides in the classroom and find new ways to help level the path that scientists were traversing in their research to find cures. I entered the PhD program in sociology at Stony Brook University knowing exactly what I wanted to study. I had seen how the United States' policy on embryonic stem cell research was highly impacted by factors entirely unrelated to the science itself, or to the potential it had for biomedical discovery. I had believed, at one point in my life, that the value and ethics of science could largely speak for themselves and that any area of scientific inquiry that was ethically sound and had the potential to revolutionize a field like medicine or energy or agriculture or astronomy would not only be permitted but encouraged. This was not the case for stem cell research, despite acknowledgments by many scientists that it was among the greatest potential applications to medicine since the discovery of antibiotics. But stem cell research had become a political issue, and like nearly all political issues, there were factions and interests across U.S. culture that were preventing the research's progression. I wanted to better understand these forces and to see if this was a uniquely U.S. situation or if other countries experienced something similar.

For my PhD dissertation, I wanted to study the impact that different cultural histories, groups, and interests had on stem cell research policymaking in countries around the world. From one country to another, there was an immense amount of variability in what embryonic stem cell research policy measures permitted or restricted, and I wanted to understand how social institutions and special-interest groups like the Catholic Church, the pharmaceutical industry, patient advocacy groups, and the scientific establishment itself impacted the policy developments and outcomes. There were not many countries around the world that had adopted a clear or formal stem cell policy, but since I was undertaking a comparative historical analysis, I had to broaden my analysis beyond just the United States. I decided that I would study the embryonic stem cell research policies in the United States, United Kingdom, Germany, and China—essentially writing four mini dissertations in one.

I spent 2011 and 2012 conducting research for my doctoral dissertation—poring through historical documents, policy statements, speeches, and science protocols. Through my research, I had found that the diversity and variability in embryonic stem cell research policies across countries was as different as their cultural histories were. I learned that policy outcomes—even for a specialized area of public policy as niche as stem cell research policy—are highly influenced by the demands that special interests and money have in political decision-making—so much so that it influences the very authority and legitimacy that we ascribe to disciplines like science or the people who practice it. And I learned that when you set your sights on achieving something, the strength of motivation and determination are not easily beaten, even when obstacles seem too overwhelming or when you feel like hope is lost.

The office in my home where I would do most of my dissertation writing is peppered with Christopher Reeve memorabilia of various kinds. I have Superman figurines and *Somewhere in Time* pocket watch replicas. I have articles about our friendship, and I have photos of Chris and me, sitting side by side in New Orleans, where *The Brooke Ellison Story* was filmed. Chris's images, some staring right back at me from my desk, were part of what kept me driven during even the bleakest days. After the horseback riding accident that would leave Chris paralyzed in 1994, he committed himself to using the resources available to him and the deep-seated humanitarian aspects of his character to commit himself to finding a treatment for spinal cord injury. Founding the Christopher and

Dana Reeve Foundation to fund scientists conducting spinal cord injury research, Chris became an indomitable fighter for the field of regenerative medicine, focusing on regeneration of neurons and other neurological cell types to treat an injured spinal cord. Chris was unafraid to hold both scientists and policymakers accountable for any rate-limiting factors that were impeding progress toward finding a cure for spinal cord injury, criss-crossing the country and traveling around the globe, speaking to the field's best and brightest, holding their feet to the fire and demanding results. Chris was a fighter in every way that he had to fight, and in many more ways than most ever have to.

When Chris passed away in 2004, he left the planet without getting to see the conclusion of the work he had started. Chris gave a face and voice not simply to spinal cord injury but also to the types of treatments that many people who live with spinal cord injury hope to see, and when he passed away it felt, for me, like I had lost a hero who was championing my cause in more than one way, a hero who did not get to see the culmination of some of the work he had started. So, when I would look at his photo or figurine, I would talk to him. I would be reminded of the work he had started and how I wanted to move it forward in some meaningful way. I would thank him for the ways he changed my life and how I hoped he would be proud of the life I was living.

But my commitment to seeing my PhD through to its completion was not just due to Chris or the role he played in my life. My drive, my passion, and my feeling of purpose—all needed to successfully account for the blood and tears that stain so many pages of dissertations—came from all the people who had contacted me over the years, sharing stories about their lives and the struggles that they or their family members had faced. With every word I wrote and every line that gave life to each page, I was accompanied by the voices of fellow soldiers in this battle. It was an academic exercise, but it was also a personal statement about the path I wanted to pave and the future I wanted to help create.

Dissertations are not only written but must also be defended. Publicly. In other words, a PhD student's contribution to intellectual thought has to be upheld against the questions, comments, and analysis of other experts in the field, in a setting in which the dissertation writer presents her work, only to be met with a series of questions probing the methodology behind the work and implications of it. A dissertation defense is a momentous and incredibly satisfying day. It's an opportunity to share your work and knowledge with people who care about the same things and, as the defense is open to the public, with people like friends, family, and colleagues. In March 2012, I defended my PhD dissertation, "Lifelines: Stem Cell Research in a Globalized World." My research drew upon so many of the skills I had learned as a master's student and knowledge I had gained from my sociology instructors—stakeholder analyses, policy construction, persuasion, culture, and the sociology of scientific knowledge. But it also brought me into a world in which policy and ethics have not only intersected but collided. Conducting this research laid the groundwork for how I would immerse myself in these areas for years to come.

Even more than that, though, my entrance into the stem cell field stood as my first real exercise of leadership. Inserting myself into the thick of the stem cell debate forced me to challenge myself in ways I never had anticipated, subjecting myself to amounts of scrutiny with which I had never before been comfortable and levels of controversy from which I may have previously run. But it was empowering. Through my involvement in stem cell research, and other important issues to follow, I was seated at the boardroom table, was given the chance to speak to global leaders of many kinds, could take part in conversations and decision-making that directly impacted me, as a disabled woman, as well as many others who live with disability. My entrance into the debate surrounding stem cell research, and taking an active stance on behalf of something about which I cared deeply, taught me that there is strength to be found in the fight, and that this strength does not go unnoticed. It was because of my work in this field that I received an honorary degree from Rutgers University. It was because of this work that I was chosen to be a Young Global Leader in the World Economic Forum and a member of the Truman National Security Project. It was because of this work that I spoke in front of thought leaders and decision-makers at the highest levels in a teleconference to Davos, Switzerland. But much more importantly, it was because of this work that I have come into contact with some of the most brilliant minds I could ever imagine knowing, people who have dedicated their talents to alleviating the suffering of others. Scientists, policymakers, philanthropists, businesspeople, advocates, family members, all using their lives, positions, and experiences to broaden minds and restore lives. It has been an honor to join these forces, a privilege to fight alongside them.

Studying and writing about the ethics of science, especially complex science that has the potential to revolutionize the world if done properly and if supported in the way that it should be, was never a vision I had for my life, at least not a strong one. But I have come to see stem cell research and my place within this debate as something bigger than science—though I am a lover of science—or advocacy—and I love to be a voice for change when change is needed. I have come to view this issue as a manifestation of the ways that we appreciate diverse points of view and how we can and must find ways to work together to solve complex problems, especially those that affect the lives of people facing devastating disease or disability. Becoming a member of this field did not mirror the expectations I had for my life, but it is where I found myself, and I am so much richer for it.

It is impossible to predict where our lives are headed. It's a fool's errand even to try. There are no road maps or street signs that guide our way, and the best we can do is hope that the road we ultimately travel resembles the road we envisioned. It is disorienting when these two do not overlap—when the vision we have for our lives bears no resemblance to the events that ultimately unfold, but who are we to say that one is better or more correct than the other? Our lives are created in the instant that we experience them, and we can choose to make them as vivid and as bold as we desire. We can shudder from or embrace the unpredictability of where our lives lead because, sometimes in that unpredictability, we find ourselves in places and seizing opportunities we, ourselves, might have never fathomed.

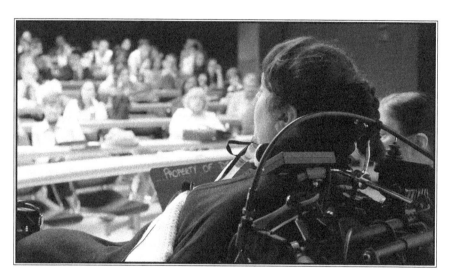

Brooke giving a lecture at the Harvard Stem Cell Institute, 2016.
(Photo by Todd Leatherman)

10

←————→

THE PROFESSOR

Despite what was expected, I have lived. I have thrived.

STONY BROOK UNIVERSITY AND THE hospital that is housed on its campus are viewable from miles away. When you take the ferry from Port Jefferson on Long Island to Bridgeport, Connecticut, the university buildings are among the last to fade into the distance as you leave the Long Island shore. It is a cornerstone of the island's social fabric and economy, and its concrete buildings provide an assurance that there is something solid and strong supporting Long Island's well-being.

It is impossible for me to talk about my life without also talking about Stony Brook University. The two are intertwined to the point of inseparability. Long Island's Nicolls Road transects the East and West Campuses of the university in the very same way that it transects my life. The symbolism has never been lost on me. If it were not for the proximity of

Stony Brook University Hospital to the site of my accident, a distance of only several hundred feet, I know I would not be alive today. The physicians, nurses, and health-care team who tended to my broken, seemingly irreparable eleven-year-old body were the creditors to a debt that I could never repay, and that has always been the case. To this day, traveling down Nicolls Road and seeing the hospital on its flanks, I still look into the windows and telegraph my own life and memories into the rooms on the other side. It is almost as if a part of me is still lying in one of the hospital beds inside.

It was within the walls of Stony Brook University Hospital, though, that my family was told that my life would be severely compromised and that we all should expect the worst in terms of what I would be able to do. This was not an unreasonable prognosis to make—in fact, likely any physician treating a patient in a condition like mine would likely say the same. The damage done to my body brought me much closer to death than to the promise of life, and the injuries that affected essentially every part of my body predicted a life that would not amount to much possibility or opportunity. That is the likely diagnosis and the safe wager, given the odds.

Even under the best possible circumstances, considering the injuries I had undergone, my future looked quite bleak. Little was known, at that time, about quadriplegia or ventilator dependence except that people did not live very long with either one, let alone both. The aesthetic surrounding disability in 1990 was very much one of exclusion and isolation, with an American society that still had not yet adopted the ideas of accessibility or adaptability—and certainly not inclusion—when it came to accommodating the lives of people with disabilities. The prediction that my life would not go far or last long required no particular talent or tarot cards. But over two decades after receiving these diagnoses and prognoses, I returned to Stony Brook University Hospital, having lived a life richer and more steeped in experience than anyone would have wagered all those years ago. Years after my accident, I returned to Stony Brook University Hospital, not as a patient but as a professor.

My office sits on the second floor of the Health Sciences Center, in the School of Health Technology and Management, in the same building that served as my makeshift home for six weeks when I was a child. It is a modest yet comfortable office, painted a soothing pastel green and adorned with *Game of Thrones* paraphernalia of all kinds. Years ago, when I was eleven years old and lying in the hospital bed several floors above, completely immobile and without any ability to breathe, it was nearly unfathomable that, years later, I would be sitting in front of a desk in the very same building. One of the PhD students with whom I have worked as a faculty member was my primary nurse when I was a child in the pediatric intensive care unit. She was my favorite nurse who cared for me there: warm, compassionate, skilled, patient. She is still all these things, yet I interact with her as a colleague, not as her patient. One of the respiratory care therapists who teaches in my school and whose office is right around the corner was the respiratory therapist who set up and attached me to my first ventilator when I was just eleven years old. Both people, whom I remember so vividly from when I was a child, rode with me in the ambulance from Stony Brook to Children's Specialized Hospital in New Jersey for rehabilitation. They saw me at my worst and cared for me at their best. And though I never expected I would be working alongside them, they have never left the place they held in my heart.

I enter the Stony Brook University Hospital building each day not to receive medical information but to provide it. I teach and study medical ethics, a subject matter to which all health-care professionals are exposed but which not all fully internalize. The term "ethics" tends not to evoke tremendous excitement or enthusiasm when seen on paper, but the topics in the courses I teach touch upon some of the most thought-provoking and challenging questions that can be asked in the fields of medicine and health care—it is a treasure trove for the curious, a haven for the thoughtful, and a land mine for the narrowminded.

Medicine is simply fraught with complex ethical questions that challenge our most fundamental sensibilities. Medicine finds us at our most vulnerable, when the infirmity in one aspect of our lives seems to cast shadows on all parts of our lives, when uncertainty and fear about what might lie ahead or inside can limit our ability to comprehend even the simplest information being shared with us. But for physicians and other health-care professionals, expertise in determining the right diagnosis does not always imply expertise in managing the intricacies of the relationship between health-care provider and patient—information giver and information receiver, potential savior and hopeful survivor. That is— or ought to be—where medical ethics finds its home, in the distance between the care that medicine can provide and the comfort that people find in that care.

The first time I stepped in front of the lecture hall, it was reminiscent of speeches I had given over the years but was in many ways very different—I was not simply sharing my life with those in front of me but trying to explain something much more abstract and complex. I was teaching Professional Ethics in Healthcare to undergraduate students who were going to pursue careers in the allied health professions, professions like physical therapy, nursing, respiratory care, occupational therapy, and physician assistant—professions I, throughout my life, had far more experience with than I often choose to discuss. The lecture hall was large but not enormous, with red stadium-style seats and desks that progressed over a good ten or fifteen rows. The university's commitment to racial, ethnic, and geographic diversity had its fulcrum in a class like mine, as most of my students came from backgrounds historically underrepresented in the health-care field. As undergraduates, many of whom had not yet realized that they could develop their own opinions on highly controversial issues, students entered the classroom not at all sure what it would be about or how their thoughts might evolve.

I am a medical ethicist with a profound physical disability. The language of disability and the language of medical ethics have a great deal of overlap in vocabulary but only minimal overlap in definition. Medical ethicists and disability advocates often talk about the same things, but they have vastly different understandings of them. Medical ethics puts academic and intellectual parameters around the experiences that people in the most challenging medical conditions encounter, often people with disabilities. In essence, medical ethics intellectualizes and debates the very real and lived experiences that people with disabilities grapple with every day. Even more than that, though, medical ethics can sometimes attempt to place a normative judgment on these experiences or aspects of existence that people with disabilities have already incorporated into their lives. So, there is a divide that is often felt by at least half of these two groups in terms of how challenging medical ethical questions are presented and discussed, a divide that has alienated one group from the other in sometimes uncomfortable ways.

I sit at a rather privileged nexus of patient and professor—a patient of some of the most unimaginable medical challenges to be found in the health-care field and a professor of a field that studies these very medical challenges. This is a remarkably rare position to find oneself, as most people who undergo medical challenges like I have—brain injury, perceptions of medical futility, technological dependence, quadriplegia, cardiopulmonary arrest—often do not live to talk about them. Far fewer live to study them. Living on both sides of this diametric opposition has allowed me to understand particularities that may not be understood by many ethicists, and it also helps me to understand the rationale and value behind positions that have been taken on challenging issues that some in the disability community have expressed outrage over. These two camps of individuals are often at vicious odds with one another, sometimes understandably, but this acrimonious relationship need not be the case. In fact, there is a great deal that can be learned by both sides when the barrier between intellectual expertise and personal sensibilities is reduced. But I sit at this unlikely and unusual intersection, and the view from one vantage point has shaped the view from the other. And I have been able to share this hybrid, or multiplicative, perspective with my students in a way that I think few others can. I can look at many of these debates from both ways.

I have no doubt that when students enter the classroom and they see an individual with quadriplegia behind the podium, they either aren't sure if they're in the right place or if I'm in the wrong place. This is an unfortunate but not unexpected reaction, as there are simply and regrettably very few people with quadriplegia in the classroom, on either side of the podium. My classrooms are on the lower floors of the hospital, so I imagine some think I'm lost or am some renegade patient trying to make an escape. But I begin each semester sharing with my students some of my life and how I found my way into the field. When we talk about medical futility, we talk about conditions like persistent vegetative states and brain death, and why there is a point in the lead-up to these diagnoses when no amount of additional care would be effective. But we also talk about the gut-wrenching struggle that families must confront when deciding what to do when that point is reached. When we talk about physician aid in dying, we talk about the dignity that is found in allowing an individual who is suffering to determine when and how her life might reach its end.

But we also talk about how the potential thoughts to end one's life are not always based on the likelihood of impending death—which, ethically speaking, they should be—but rather sometimes because of socially fixable circumstances, like loneliness or inopportunity or poverty or lack of community, and how in instances like these, we as a society should be doing all that we can to address them so that ending one's life is the last choice. In my class, we talk about the ethics of genetics research and how advances in this field might reduce the likelihood of a couple passing along histories of genetic predisposition to disease to their children, but we also talk about what conversations about the eradication of disease and disability mean to people who live with them, how conversations, if not constructed properly, can lead people already living difficult lives to believe that society would be better off without them. These arguments exist at opposing sides of the debate, yet each is worth discussing; each has its place in the contour of our conversations.

This is a perspective that very few future health-care professionals ever receive—the perspective of the patient turned professor. It is difficult to find many people who have experienced, firsthand, the very topics that are discussed in medical ethics classes—the agony of end-of-life decision-making, the worthiness of medical care that might seem futile, the value of a life lived with severe disability and on medical technology, the complexity of physician aid in dying, and what it means for people with disabilities whose lives are often miscalculated or undervalued. But there is a benefit in having these conversations from a spectrum of positions, and the impact of this personal experience is not lost on my students. Over the years, I have received correspondences from students who have gone on to become nurses, physicians, physical therapists, and respiratory care therapists. These students share with me some of their interactions with their patients and how these have been influenced by the conversations they had in my class, how the ethics class they took with me impacted the way they understood their patients as well as the decisions their patients had to make.

I teach students at all levels—undergraduates, graduates, doctoral students, and medical students—and it is interacting with the medical students that has been the most unusual and interesting. Medical students are trained to make diagnoses based on probabilities and likelihoods, which makes sense, as those diagnoses are, by definition, the most likely. In 1990, the information that was being given to my family and me was probabilistically accurate, especially for what was known at the time about spinal cord injury and about disability in general. Likely many physicians in many places would have given my family and me the same message—that I should expect a life of deprivation and limitation. But the *physical* paralysis I was confronting did not need to be synonymous with the lack of social participation or contribution that many were expecting from my life. At the age of eleven, when children are likely to envision all sorts of opportunities and possibilities for their lives, that distinction between my body and my ability was what I needed to hear and needed to believe in.

So I have made it my quest and passion to ensure that a new generation of physicians is equipped to convey the reality and severity of a devastating diagnosis but, at the same time, remain hopeful about what life has to offer. I want physicians and health-care providers to understand the experiences that patients undergo, beyond what is documented in textbooks and in the most fragile of circumstances. I want to help ensure that physicians and health-care professionals understand not only the importance of making a diagnosis but also the importance of knowing the intricacies of a medical experience before placing judgment on it. There are things that I have experienced that I want physicians to know. There are things that I have experienced that I want people to know.

Despite what was expected, I have lived. I have thrived. I have lived as a woman with a disability and have grown to know what that means: medically and socially, personally and collectively. Contrary to what many people believe or understand, disability is not an ailment. Disability is not necessarily analogous with medical vulnerability, though it might sometimes involve it. According to many, a life like my own can fail to meet the arbitrary standard of a life worth living. Hollywood storytelling and medical history alike are laced with stories of the fallen hero—the individuals who would have led an idyllic life had they not been bested by the despair brought about by quadriplegia or immobility. It is thought to be unlivable because, in many ways, it is unimaginable—the ostensibly mummified soul, the trapped, the would-have-been.

We fear what we do not know, and there are few things more unknown than life lived without movement or sensation. It is a set of circumstances that no one would freely choose and most anyone would change for oneself. Yet, many of the presumptions made about it, or the assumed experience pursuant to it, are frighteningly off base. Third-party estimates of the relative difficulty of someone's life are notoriously inaccurate and can even have the unintended consequence of prescribing an outcome that is possibly irrelevant to the real, lived experiences at hand.

My quadriplegia is the result of a tragic accident that I was fortunate to survive. If one gains expertise through experience and exposure, our population of experts on death is small and fragile, but I count myself among them. The surprising consequence of a near-death experience is that once death has brought itself near to you, it remains there, in your thoughts and in your personhood. Death is a rare life guest that immediately overstays its welcome and stays anyway. It is almost as if a brush with death causes epigenetic changes to your DNA that become a part of your being and identity. It never goes away and remains long after the immediate risk of death has been alleviated, long after medical interventions have claimed their victory. There are times when I wish I could remember something—an image, a sensation, a perception—from the nearly two days I spent in the chasm between the here and the somewhere else, but my memory is as vacuous as what I expect that in-between to have been. There are no journal entries or holiday snaps to spark my memory of the time I tiptoed the line between life and death, and I have no stories to tell about how close my consciousness came to becoming irreversibly unconscious, but the knowledge of having stayed there and flirted with death—if even for a brief time—has breathed an ironic life into my thoughts and actions ever since.

I want physicians and health-care professionals to begin to understand what it is like to wake up in the hospital following a devastating injury. After my accident, I lingered in the undetermined space in between life and death for thirty-six hours, a duration that is interminably long for loved ones in wait yet brutally short when faced with decisions yielding long-term consequences. It is a time without feeling, a structureless existence with Dali-esque surrealism. But I awoke. I awoke to the alarms produced by the willful resistance I was forcing against a ventilator pushing air into my lungs. I have staggeringly vivid and detailed memories of the days I was willing my way back to life, perhaps only partially alive. I had terrifyingly little faith in the machine keeping me alive, understood each forced breath—coming either too quickly or not quickly enough—as a violation to my body and sensibilities. It is jarringly uncomfortable and unsettling to breathe in a mechanized fashion, at a prescribed rate, at neither a pace nor volume of your own choosing, and I remember fighting against it, against what I perceived to be the most tangible and immediate foe I could try to wrestle to the ground. I was never taught to breathe without breathing or how to outsource the most fundamentally natural, in-house skill to someone or something else. I was never taught how the rhythmic and regulated pace of breath that lies at the foundation of meditation and serenity can feel anything but meditative or serene. No one tells you how it will feel because essentially no one who is in the position to tell you has ever actually felt it. But what I was also not taught was that this machine, this foreign object that I intrinsically wanted to reject almost immunologically, was not my true foe and that my will to fight was misplaced—misdirected to the ventilator, when my will to fight needed to be reserved for the recovery ahead.

I want to help ensure that physicians, health-care professionals, and family members of patients understand and can assist in the creation of nuanced and evolutionary visions of recovery for a patient, and how deeply embedded this concept is in the vantage point from the hospital bed. Recovery: a word uttered with justifiable trepidation in the medical field. Recovery: the logical antithesis of futility. Moving from unconsciousness to consciousness, intensive care to rehabilitation, I had no clear or even realistic idea of what recovery would look like for me on either a short-term or long-term scale. I understood "recovery" to be what so many of us understand it to be—a state defined by restoration and retrospective wholeness, which can obscure the different or more modest changes that no less define recovery. I have not "recovered" from quadriplegia or ventilator dependence, at least not in the way that many would reflexively interpret it. My body still lacks mobility and sensation below an indistinguishable point in my neck. My lungs still receive the air I need for survival through a tracheostomy operationalized through its yards of plastic tubing connected to a ventilator. These things have not changed, and whether or not they ever will bears no reflection on how I understand myself to have recovered.

Just as in any other general medical ethics course, in my courses, we discuss comas and persistent vegetative states, and for many students, these concepts are as foreign and unrelatable as the most arcane theories of quantum mechanics. The assigned cases are riveting but remote, bafflingly personal and impersonal at the same time, and sometimes they are presented in such a way that allows for analysis that favors a harsh medical calculus over a more human approach. And in part because of this unrelatability and seeming irrelevance to their lives, many of my students have viewed it initially as a purely medical aberration, sterilized and anesthetized like a preoperative protocol. Yet there are stories behind these concepts, real lives behind these concepts that are sometimes easily kept out of mind when they are not in sight. There are families like mine grieving with the weight of life's most agonizing decisions. So to complement the classic cases we read, I discuss what my family underwent when being told that their daughter and sister likely would not live or would not have any ability to interact with the world, how the yearning to see one live and the unspoken hope for reprieve that immediately causes shame can exist coincidentally. I share how my parents were immediately thrust into a world they did not recognize and were exposed to a language they did not understand as they tried to envision their lives either with or without their daughter. I share how my sister, brother, and extended family waited with contradictory hope and dread for news, knowing that even the best of news could only be so good. And I share how a family can move forward—how the effects of a devastating accident or disease are felt across everyone in different ways but how they can ultimately become just life once again.

Just like any other general bioethics course, in my courses, we discuss physician aid in dying, and how the right to end one's life at the time of one's own choosing has become so deeply enmeshed in debates about personhood, our societal visions of physical impairment, and our fundamental understandings of civil liberties. In the context of this discussion, each semester I ask my students—with neither expectation nor judgment—their thoughts on what might constitute a life not worth living. Understandably, some students answer relationally, saying that they would not want to live without the comfort of friends and family. However, invariably, there are many others who answer more tangibly and behaviorally, saying that they could not live if they were to lack independence, or if they could not engage in the physical activities that give their lives meaning, or if they were attached to machines and tubes, or even if they were paralyzed and could not use their bodies in the same way they had. But throughout the course of the semester, we invariably discuss the parts of disease and disability that are *medical in nature*, like physical pain, secondary infection, autonomic dysreflexia, and loss of function, and the parts that are *societal in nature*, like social marginalization, unemployment, poverty, and loss of independence. We discuss how the confluence of both types of factors impact an overall quality of life, and how the former can be managed or adapted to, and how the latter can be alleviated if we, as a society, work to do it. In sharing what it is like to live with extreme physical limitation, I have seen many students evolve in their thinking and reach the conclusion that life can be and often is rich and full of meaning even when much has been lost. They come to the awareness that we can respect individual choice and autonomous decision-making, especially when life is reaching its conclusion, but that we also can work together as a society to provide opportunity and resources so that a life-ending decision is not necessarily the most obvious decision.

These are key lessons—among the most important to my own recovery over the past three decades—that are in no way included in medical or even bioethical textbooks, and these are lessons that health-care professionals ought to know. I share how, when one undergoes disease or disability, it is easy to feel as if the journey that is taken is a journey taken alone—that the diagnosis implicitly creates an isolation between a sense of normality enjoyed by most and a sense of abnormality put on the shoulders of a penalized few. It is also easy to feel as though the magnitude of the diagnosis is all-encompassing, circumscribing every aspect of life at all times. Yet none of these assumptions is necessarily true; neither of these feelings of hopelessness is a sequela brought about by the diagnosis. While it is not the physician's given responsibility to change these perceptions of oneself in the context of disease, it is the hallmark of the exceptional physician.

In my position as both patient and professor, I have come to understand that I have also been a student. In my own personal reflections of my experiences as an educator, I have gained a new understanding and method by which to articulate the intricacies of my life. In this idiosyncratic intersectionality in which I reside, I have been forced to look at my own life through a sometimes uncomfortable bioethical lens, counterbalancing what I know to be true about my own life with what I also know to be true about many others'. I have worked to disaggregate personal anecdotal experience from generalizable occurrence while giving enough value to each to make them useful for future health-care providers. I have been challenged to think more deeply about the insidious ways that trauma affects our lives but how we can become more resilient by putting it to positive use. These opportunities to think more deeply about questions that far too few ever want to think about at all have been gifts for my students and me, in equal measure.

While there are many, though not enough, personal accounts of the doctor turned patient, accounts of the reverse directionality are staggeringly uncommon. For me, it can be a unique and sometimes disorienting experience to read scholarly works and articulately intellectualized theories surrounding complex medical and personal decision-making that I not only experienced years ago but will continue to experience for the rest of my life. The life I lead and professional position I hold are dichotomous yet complementary. The science and art of medicine—the wisdom behind it and the care to provide it—are two halves of the same whole, two hemispheres of the brain, each of which has difficulty functioning to its greatest effect without the other. The duality of this relationship has been much easier to understand and then teach after having lived through it.

These are the questions I focus on both in my instruction and in my writing: how best to synthesize the care that patients want with the care that physicians provide, and these two circles of a Venn diagram do not uniformly overlap. When medicine becomes as central a part of one's life as it has to mine, you realize that there is an art to the practice, and a broad spectrum of excellence in this art. Since the advent of antibiotics, when the curative (as opposed to the maintenance) characteristic of medicine began to evolve, a movement toward health-care quality likewise took hold, with evidence-based practice and probabilistic diagnoses sitting at its heart. There is—and rightly so—perhaps no one who would argue against the evidence-based and probabilistic framework in which medicine is practiced today. Great physicians know this, and many great physicians practice accordingly. Yet, the true mastery of medicine necessarily includes but also exceeds the ability to make the best and most educated diagnosis the majority of the time. Excellence in the true art of medicine, as anyone who has spent significant amounts of time in the company of physicians can attest, lies also in the compassion and empathy they can offer their patients: the ability to perform lifesaving medical feats but also the capacity to understand a family's grief and uncertainty while these feats are being performed; the ability to make the judgment as to when life support might be necessary but the compassion to learn what a life lived on life support is truly like; the skill to make a difficult diagnosis but also the sensitivity to deliver it with hope. In my years living through some of the most unenviable health circumstances, I know how important these conjoined skills are, how rarely they are jointly implemented, and how physicians and health-care providers can embrace both without sacrificing either. Providing the best and right diagnosis for a patient sits alongside establishing the best, most compassionate, and most hopeful relationship with a patient. This is expertise also brought about by experience and exposure.

Many people could say that they would not be alive were it not for the advances of modern medicine. But I would not be here were it not for medicine at its most complex and aggressive. I am indebted both to science and to the medicine it produces. But who I am as an individual and what I have found the strength within myself to achieve was not the outcome of medicine, it was the outcome of compassion and empathy and fostering of hope when circumstances seemed bleakest. Though this may not be articulated in textbooks, there is nothing more significant than this; there is no greater gift that a physician can provide to her patients.

When I am navigating the halls of Stony Brook University Hospital, I do it most often from the vantage point of a professor and, sometimes, from the perspective of a patient. But even as a professor, the understandings I have about medicine and patient care were only achieved through *being* a patient. It is indistinguishable from who I am. And I am deeply thankful for that. I typically don't like to imagine hypotheticals or "counterfactuals" in terms of what my life would have been like, but I know that my current life as a scholar and my work enriching the experiences of future physicians would be far less meaningful were it not for my life as a patient.

11

←——————→

THE LESSON

My life is what it is not despite what I have undergone,
it is what it is because of what I have undergone.

I DON'T REMEMBER THE PRECISE moment I woke up. The more
I think about it, the more I suspect it was an evolutionary waking-up
process—isolated moments of awareness followed by an understanding,
then an acceptance, and then a growth. The emergence of my identity
as a woman with quadriplegia and ventilator dependence was evolutionary, yet nevertheless revolutionary because every part of me—the person
I had once been and had understood myself to be—was afraid of it, felt
diminished by it, and fundamentally undervalued it. But in those inter-
pretations, I was viewing my life in a wrong, or at least incomplete, way.
Looking at it in retrospect, I have come to see that my life was branded
by the isolated trauma of my accident and the significance of my resulting

disability; these are inseparable and even beautiful parts of who I am. But they are not all of who I am. My life has been branded by tragedy, but who I am today, the strength that I have found and the identity I have based my existence on, is the product of the moments of unrelenting hope, the opportunities for pristine love, and the times when I was brought to my knees in heartache or pain but still summoned the will to fight on. These isolated moments are not *caused* by disability, but they are framed by it—moments that I now see as the trajectory of my identity, years in the making but invisible to me thirty years ago.

There is very little that makes sense when you're eleven years old, and a newly acquired disability like quadriplegia is no exception. But the acquisition of a disability like quadriplegia does not make sense at *any* point in life. Over the years, my life and experiences have brought me into contact with people from all parts of the world who have been in accidents or encountered disease that left them paralyzed at all points of life, and not once have I heard that this transition was an easy one. Undoubtedly, people can continue with their lives and can go on to achieve unimaginable things, but it is almost never the case that the transition from a life lived without disability to a life with disability is easy, smooth, or without pain.

I am in my fourth decade living with quadriplegia. Paralysis has contextualized my existence for three times longer than it hasn't, and yet, it still feels new sometimes. I have heard it said that the average life span of someone with quadriplegia—bear in mind, not *ventilator-dependent* quadriplegia but just run-of-the-mill quadriplegia—is seven years post-accident. Of course, I understand that this average is likely reduced considerably by those who don't survive at all following a paralyzing accident, as well as by those who are without the resources or supports to live very long, but one way or the other, the number is staggeringly small. I have also heard it said that paralysis ages your body at a rate of seven times that of everyone else. On those data alone, my more-than-thirty years living with quadriplegia is unlikely—the statistical anomaly that seems much more astonishing in the abstract than it does in the day-to-day. Such is the nature of existence though, really—an astounding feat when looked at telescopically, much more mundane when looked at microscopically.

For most of my life, I have been fortunate to consider myself disabled but not necessarily sick. However, over the span of the past few years, as my body has aged and absorbed all the deviations from the typical that quadriplegia enforces, I have felt and come to accept the realities that my story will reach its natural conclusion on a timeline vastly shorter than most others my age. I am not especially pleased about that expectation, as there are experiences that I hope to have, nephews I want to watch grow, and changes I hope to see in the world that have not changed yet. I'm not especially pleased about that expectation, but I'm not afraid of it. I have no more regrets over the life that has brought me to where I am than anyone else does over theirs. Perhaps I will live another thirty years with or maybe even without quadriplegia, and though I consider that to be unlikely, I have snarled in the face of the unlikely before and I am not hesitant to do it again. But over the past few years, as the line between disability and illness has begun to bleed, I see more of my life behind me than in front of me. Nonetheless, I continue to look both ways.

There are times when I look back on my life and see it for all the negative space it contains, all the ways that it is made visible by what it lacks. It is almost as if it is a human predisposition to do this—to look at our lives and see what is not there, all the parts that would, if present, make us more complete and bring us closer to our true selves. But there is addition in the subtraction. My life is what it is not *despite* what I have undergone, it is what it is *because* of what I have undergone. I can look at the negative space and consider it hollowness or I can look at the negative space and see the light that it captures.

My life has been unlike any other, but I suppose, in that regard, it makes it just like anyone else's. At the same time, my life has not been typical or average; it has been the summation of wildly deviating extremes—experiencing half of them would be noteworthy, but all of them, quite spectacular. As I sit in my office in the Health Sciences Center of Stony Brook University as a tenured associate professor of medical and science ethics, I think about my broken body that was alive in only the most minimal ways, lying in a hospital bed only several floors above. The shortness of the physical distance only serves to magnify the length of the personal distance. The words that I speak as a professor are a reflection of the experiences I had as a patient, training students who will soon walk the same hospital corridors that my parents and family did so many years ago. It is my hope that my words and experiences will be spoken through these new physicians to comfort other patients and other families who are as fearful as my family and I were about what lies on the road ahead. I think about the children who sat by my side in their wheelchairs in front of the nurses' station at Children's Specialized Hospital, and I juxtapose them with my classmates who sat next to me in lecture halls of Harvard University. While the predicted or expected distinction between the two might be staggering, the actual functional role that each played in my life is much less so. I am who I am today as a result of the conversations I had about philosophy and science with my Harvard classmates just as I am who I am today as a result of the conversations I had about learning to get through each day as a child with a disability with the children who lived in the hospital with me. I think about speeches I have given to and conversations I have had with some of the most influential decision-makers and stakeholders in the world today, yet any member of any of these audiences is powerless in combating the greatest threats to my life right now—infection, exhaustion, pressure, atrophy. The positions we believe we hold in some arbitrary and constructed social hierarchy have no bearing on the myriad ways we are vulnerable in our humanness. But at the same time, I realize the unifying nature of our humanness is not exclusive to our vulnerability or the ways in which we suffer. Our humanness is that much more unifying in the ways we protect those we believe to be vulnerable, in the ways we bring comfort to those who suffer, and the ways we can either wither or thrive depending on the precise arrangements of each of these.

My life has been one of trauma, but it is also one of recovery. My life has been one of devastation, but it is also one of exhilaration. My life has been one of loss, but it is also one of achievement. My life has been one of heartbreak, but it is also one of love. The trauma that humans undergo when they become disabled is a physical, albeit extreme, manifestation of trauma that humans undergo by virtue of being human. All of our trauma and times of difficulty are inflection points in our lives, times when we are forced to make choices we do not want to make, choices that change the way we live our lives and that test the deepest parts of our sense of resolve. Irrespective of the path we choose—a path paved by fear and heartache or a path paved by hope and resilience—we are never the people we expect ourselves to be. We can never simply return to things as they were or believe that the way they were was the way they ought to be. The changes and traumas we experience, essentially by definition, change the vantage point from which we can understand ourselves. They don't necessarily give us the opportunity to isolate silver linings or make lemonade where lemons were before, but they do allow us to see the world differently. They allow us to have an additional dimension from which to decipher the complexity of the human experience, to understand more about the lives of people we may never have even thought about before, to understand more of the many ways that life can bring people to their knees, to see more of the ways that people find the will to get back on their feet. What my life has lost in the breadth of experience, it has gained, manifold, in its depth. Colors are richer, if not as many. Years of my life are fuller, if maybe fewer. And love is stronger, without any additional qualification.

I would never claim that trauma or pain or challenge is the necessary antecedent to life viewed from more discerning angles. Nor is the former the prescribed outcome of the latter. We do not need pain to be deeper people, and depth of character is certainly not the definitive outcome of having undergone pain. But it can be. And that is perhaps the biggest lesson I have learned in my life, and perhaps the biggest accomplishment over which I can claim credit. Pain and struggle do not prescribe any particular outcome—neither one of deeper understanding nor less understanding—but either is equally possible despite what we are told is probable. Individually and, when we are fortunate enough, together, we have many of the virtues we need to withstand more than we might ever think we could, to fight back when we feel like all is lost, to find meaning and purpose when we think there is none, to care longer and more intensely than we ever thought was possible, to take on odds stacked strongly against us, and to find ourselves still standing in whatever way we can on the other side. I cannot think of a more valuable lesson than that. I cannot think of a better way to look at my life when I look at it from any direction. As a child, I was taught to look both ways, as if there were only two. I realize now that we need to look all ways. Always.

ACKNOWLEDGMENTS

←———————→

LOOK BOTH WAYS IS AS personal and as honest a work as I can imagine myself writing. However, a book about the intricacies of my own life, identity, and the lessons therein necessarily implies the incorporation of the people who have made my life and this work what they have become. I'd like to acknowledge:

My parents, Edward and Jean, who are the very backbone of all that I do and whose unshakable support has given me not only the opportunities but also the empowerment to live my life as fully as I have. I love you, and I don't know how you do what you do.

Kysten and Reed, who have walked on both sides of me throughout my life for as long as I have lived it, never questioning the turns we have had to take or the changes we have had to make. I love you, and I couldn't imagine a better pair of siblings to grow up with.

Stephanie Viola, whose brilliance and literary talent brought this book through the editing and promotion process. You have made this possible, without asking for anything in return, and have brought it from words on a page to a reality. *Look Both Ways* would not exist were it not for you.

Angela Morelli, whose gift for seeing the world in more spectacular and unexpected ways conceived of this cover and brought it to life. Your beauty and spirit are reflected in all that you say and all you create.

Christine Carrion, whose photographic talent and decades of friendship framed the photo on the front cover.

Trisha Thompson, who saw the value in this book and ensured that the world had the opportunity to see it.

My friends and family who have made my life and all of the events in it either more bearable when they were difficult or more beautiful when they were not. I love you more than I can quantify or, despite my love for words, could ever fully articulate.

Top: Brooke, age nine, outside the U.S. Capitol, visiting Washington, D.C., 1988. Bottom: Brooke at the Capitol, speaking on behalf of the Christopher and Dana Reeve Paralysis Act, July 2006.

NOTES

1   Ellison, B. 2019. The Patient as Professor: How My Life as a Person with Quadriplegia Shaped My Thinking as an Ethicist. *Perspectives in Biology and Medicine.* 62 (2), pp. 342–351. DOI: 10.1353/pbm.2019.0018

2   Goleman, D. 1995. *Emotional Intelligence: Why It Can Matter More Than IQ.* Bantam Books. New York, New York.

3   Merton, R. 1968. *Social Theory and Social Structure.* The Free Press. New York, New York.

4   Schatz, J. L. and George, A. E. 2018. *The Image of Disability: Essays on Media Representations.* McFarland. New York, New York.

5   Caregiver Action Network. 2019. Caregiver statistics. Retrieved from: https://www.caregiveraction.org/resources/caregiver-statistics

6   Eldercare Workforce Alliance. 2018. Family Caregivers: The Backbone of Our Eldercare System. Retrieved from: https://eldercareworkforce.org/wp-content/uploads/2018/03/Caregiving_Issue_Brief_Update_FINAL.pdf

7   Chidambaram, P. 2020. State Reporting of Cases and Deaths Due to Covid-19 in Long-Term Care Facilities. Kaiser Family Foundation. Retrieved from: https://www.kff.org/coronavirus-covid-19/issue-brief/state-reporting-of-cases-and-deaths-due-to-covid-19-in-long-term-care-facilities/

8   Harrington, C., Carrillo, H., Garfield, R., and Squires, E. 2018. Nursing Facilities, Staffing, Residents, and Facility Deficiencies, 2009 through 2016. Kaiser Family Foundation. Retrieved from: https://www.kff.org/report-section/nursing-facilities-staffing-residents-and-facility-deficiencies-2009-through-2016-facility-deficiencies/

9   Goffman, E. 1986. *Stigma: Notes on the Management of a Spoiled Identity.* Simon & Schuster. New York, New York.

10   Goffman.

11   Sen, A. 1985. *Commodities and Capabilities.* Amsterdam. New York, New York.

12   World Health Organization. 2002. Towards a Common Language for Functioning, Disability, and Health. Retrieved from: https://www.who.int/classifications/icf/icfbeginnersguide.pdf

13   United Nations Department of Economic and Social Affairs, Disability. 2006. Convention on the Rights of Persons with Disabilities, Article 23: Respect for home and the family. Retrieved from: https://www.un.org/development/desa/disabilities/convention-on-the-rights-of-persons-with-disabilities/article-23-respect-for-home-and-the-family.html

14   United Nations Enable. 2006. Convention on the Rights of Persons with Disabilities. Retrieved from: https://www.un.org/esa/socdev/enable/convinfopara.htm

15   Disability Justice. 2020. Sexual abuse. Retrieved from: https://disabilityjustice.org/sexual-abuse/

16   National Public Radio. 2018. The Sexual Assault Epidemic No One Talks About. Retrieved from: https://www.npr.org/2018/01/08/570224090/the-sexual-assault-epidemic-no-one-talks-about

17   Feder, A., Charney, D., and Collins, K. 2011. "Neurobiology of resilience," in S. Southwick, B. Litz, D. Charney, & M. Friedman (Eds.), *Resilience and Mental Health: Challenges Across the Lifespan* (pp. 1–29). Cambridge University Press. Cambridge. DOI:10.1017/CBO9780511994791.003

18   Kahneman, D. 2011. *Thinking Fast and Slow.* Farrar, Straus, and Giroux. New York, New York.

19 Unger, R. and West, C. 1998. *The Future of American Progressivism*. Beacon Press. Boston, Massachusetts.

20 Feder, et al.

21 Tabibnia, G. and Radecki, D. 2018. Resilience Training That Can Change the Brain. *Consulting Psychology Journal: Practice and Research*. 70 (1): 59–88.

22 Disability Status Report. 2019. Retrieved from: https://disabilitystatistics.org/reports/acs.cfm?statistic=1

23 Schur, L. and Kruse, D. 2021. Disability and Voting Accessibility in the 2020 Elections: Final Report on Survey Results. Rutgers University, Program for Disability Research. Retrieved from: https://www.eac.gov/sites/default/files/voters/Disability_and_voting_accessibility_in_the_2020_elections_final_report_on_survey_results.pdf

24 National Council on Independent Living. 2018. Candidates with Disabilities Running for Elected Office. Retrieved from: https://ncil.org/candidates/

25 Hunt, V., Layton, D., and Prince, S. 2015. Why Diversity Matters. McKinsey and Company. Retrieved from: https://www.mckinsey.com/~/media/mckinsey/business%20functions/organization/our%20insights/why%20diversity%20matters/why%20diversity%20matters.pdf

26 Fisher, R. and Ury, W. 2011. *Getting to Yes: Negotiating Agreement without Giving In*. Penguin Books. New York, New York.

ABOUT THE AUTHOR

←——————→

Brooke after getting her "Imagine" tattoo, 2008.

BROOKE ELLISON is an author, public speaker, two-time Harvard graduate, scholar, humanitarian, and survivor. Living for more than thirty years with quadriplegia, Brooke has dedicated her life to hope, resilience, and empowerment.

A policy and ethics expert in stem cell research for more than fifteen years, Brooke has been committed to changing the perception of life-saving science. From 2007 to 2014, Brooke served on the Empire State Stem Cell Board, which designed New York State's stem cell policy. As a faculty member at Stony Brook University, Brooke serves as director of the Center for Community Engagement and Leadership Development, empowering underserved communities.

The details of Brooke's life have been widely covered in publications and television programs, such as *The New York Times, People* magazine, the *Today* show, *Good Morning America*, and *Larry King Live*. In each of these appearances, Brooke has expressed her desire to have an impact on the world, stating, "Wherever there is a condition of discouragement or inopportunity, that's where I hope to be."

CPSIA information can be obtained
at www.ICGtesting.com
Printed in the USA
LVHW111746010622
720090LV00008BA/273/J